Jeffrey Dahmer:

The Terrifying Story of the
Milwaukee Cannibal (Serial
Killer True Crime)

By
James Richmond

Table of Contents

Introduction

Late into the summer night of July 22, 1991, Milwaukee police gathered inside the neat and tidy one-bedroom apartment at 924 North 25th street. A sickening smell hung in the air of apartment 213 like a chemical concoction of death and rot. Decay: an inescapable smell that bothered the neighbors as it leached through the halls. Blood soaked through the living room carpet, staining the wood planks below. A perfectly preserved head chilled in the refrigerator, and several more were stored in plastic bags within the freezer. Empty beer cans littered the table beside an opened potato chip bag and fish food. An aquarium bubbled as fish, happy and well-tended, darted around the water. Posters of male torsos were stuck to the wall.

Beyond the bedroom door, loose wires and tools were strewn around the room. A large metal pot contained decomposing hands as well as a penis. Various chemicals in the closet, including chloroform and formaldehyde, were once used to preserve male genitals inside glass jars. In the top dresser drawer were thirty polaroids of dismembered men,

1

victims staged after death: a man sliced from his head straight to his groin, a head thrown in the sink, one body completely skinned, a skeleton hanging in the closet, all positioned and poised meticulously. More skulls were found in boxes, along with a photo diary full of more nightmarish polaroids. Some were images of the victims still alive in sexual positions with handcuffs or tied up; others were gruesome snapshots of one man's dark playground.

In the corner of the bedroom, a solid blue fifty-seven-gallon barrel stood. Beneath its black plastic lid, bodies decomposed in an oozing chemical bath.

At the Milwaukee police headquarters, the owner of apartment 213 sat across from two police officers with a cigarette pressed between his lips. A heavy wall of smoke filled the interrogation room in thick and lazy puffs. It was one-thirty in the morning, and for the next six hours, Jeffrey Lionel Dahmer would confess to killing seventeen young men. Absorbed in his own distorted fantasy, he claimed to kill these men in order to keep them with him—to control them, hanging on to pieces of their body as mementos. He went as far as to eat his victims in a bid to maintain a part of them within himself.

As the horrific details leaked out, the news and media made Jeffrey Dahmer a household name. His notoriety was on par with a fictional monster like Jason Vorhees or Mike Myers. Though most know him as the cannibalistic killer, Jeffery's isolation and loneliness defined him. He was a man whose malicious fantasies were left to stew and metastasize. He did not savor the act of killing, for it was only a means to an end, to achieve his dreams. Upon death, his victims were forever his, and they could never leave him. Gay, predominantly Black men, were to Dahmer playthings, objects of fantasies for him to use as he wished. He preyed upon those looked down upon by society, whom the police had little interest in pursuing. Though many found Jeffrey strange, few if none looked at him and believed he was capable of killing.

Jeffrey was a nice boy, clean-cut and polite. He was handsome with light blonde hair and striking blue eyes, a child to a mother and father who loved him. But this normal American boy would one day create zombies in his living room and store a human head in his work locker. He was, at one time, just a normal child from Ohio, yet something, somehow, went horribly wrong. According to Jeffrey himself, "To this day, I don't know what started it. The person to blame is sitting right across from you. It's the only person. Not parents, not society, not pornography. I mean, those are just excuses."

Child Before the Monster

"When I was a little kid, I was just like anybody else," Jeffrey Dahmer reflected in an interview.

His father, Lionel Herbert Dahmer, was twenty-three years old when he married Annette Joyce Flint. The young couple's ceremony was held on August 22, 1950, and shortly after the wedding, Joyce became pregnant. The honeymoon phase for the young couple was brief; they couldn't have been more different, and a rift was forming between the two of them. Lionel was studious and stern, consumed in his work. He studied for a Bachelor of Science with a focus in chemistry at Marquette University, spending long hours in the laboratory, neglecting his young family. Joyce was emotional and suffered from the lasting trauma of an alcoholic father. She struggled with depression.

Early on in their marriage, an argument erupted between the two of them. In a fit, Joyce ran out of the house. It was close to the new year and late at night. The frigid winter air blew as Joyce marched four blocks without a coat or boots, bracing against the brutal chill until finally stopping at a bench. That is where Lionel found her.

She had been pregnant at the time.

February and March of 1960, nausea from morning sickness forced Joyce to remain in bed. She lost her job because of it. Now bedridden, her nervousness increased, and she was constantly on edge. The slightest disturbance became a bother; even the smell of their downstairs neighbor's cooking became like torture to her. Desperate to remove the stench, she begged Lionel to confront the neighbors about their cooking. He refused.

On May 21, 1960, Joyce gave birth while Lionel was at the university working. It was around five in the afternoon when he arrived to find his wife the happiest she'd been in a long time. In the hospital room, Joyce held their new baby in her arms.

"You have a son," she said. They named him Jeffrey Lionel Dahmer. Aside from wearing a cast for a minor orthopedic correction in his first four months, Jeff, as his family called him, was in excellent health.

Two weeks after he was born, they moved into Lionel's parents' house for Joyce to be more comfortable.

But the move did little to ease her. At her in-laws, she was continually subjected to nerves and nausea. A rigidness overcame her that the doctors were never able to diagnose. At times her body seized up and her legs trembled. Her eyes widened and her jaw jutted out, locking, as saliva foamed between her lips. During these nervous fits, Lionel, along with his parents, walked her around the living room to relieve the pain, but usually, it took an injection to offer what slight relief she could get. She relied on drugs to help with the pain, which pushed her deeper into isolation. Her husband remained buried in his work to escape the pressure of his wife and marriage.

Alone, Joyce's anxiety and fears became volatile. She spent more time in bed, isolated, with Jeffrey's bassinette a few feet away. When Lionel was home, the arguments and disputes continued. Joyce's behavior could be unpredictable; often, Joyce would run out of the house. One afternoon, Lionel found his wife lying in a tall grass field in nothing but her nightgown.

They moved once more, out of Lionel's parent's home and to a new apartment. All the while, their son was a typical, happy baby. Joyce remained at home while Lionel continued his studies at the university. She took care of her son's every need and walked him down the sidewalk in his stroller past ice cream shops and other homes. For the next two years, a balance finally fell over the home. The young couple had their fights, but there were also happy moments in between. But these brief respites of peace were part of a reoccurring pattern between Joyce and Lionel, and through it all, Jeffrey remained a sweet and easy baby.

In September of 1962, Lionel was offered a graduate assistant position at Iowa State University to pursue his Ph.D. Shortly after accepting, the young family moved out to Ames, Iowa. As he continued endless hours of work, the feelings of abandonment returned to Joyce. The isolation became suffocating. Her days were spent at home with Jeffrey, cleaning and cooking. Nightmares plagued her sleep, and the fighting became violent, rising in rage. At one point, Joyce snatched the kitchen knife and began to swing it at her husband wildly.

When her outbursts reached this level, Lionel escaped to work and into his studies to remain unbothered.

When Lionel would return home, Jeffrey rushed to the door, eager to meet his father with an embrace. Young Jeff loved his family. "I remember how he came thundering through the house when his grandparents came to visit," Lionel mentioned to a reporter later on. When he and Jeffrey spent time with one another, it was spent outdoors playing and exploring. Once, they rescued a nighthawk that had fallen from its nest. Jeffrey saw the bird on the hard pavement and begged his father to help take care of it. After several weeks of nursing the bird back to health, the family gathered together to witness it soar into the open blue sky.

In the late fall of 1964, after the green leaves transformed into a dusty brown and a chill began to settle in the air, Lionel Dahmer descended into the home's crawl space. He was investigating a horrid smell that was slowly growing in potency. Armed with a flashlight and bucket, he discovered a pile of rodent bones rotting beneath the floor and assumed they were killed by the local civets for food. Most similar to the skunk, civets have a nasty smell to them. Lionel gathered the bones into the bucket and emerged from the crawl space.

He spoke to Joyce about his findings, setting the bucket down. Curious, four-year-old Jeffrey peered into the bucket and with small fist-fulls of bone, tossed them on the ground. His bright blue eyes stared intently as he dropped them over and over, listening to the tapping sound in wonder.

"Like fiddlesticks," he said.

As Jeff grew, his father noticed how his son preferred certain games over others, ones that required rules and repetition. He did not like wrestling or physical matches but liked playing hide and seek or ghost in the graveyard.

In the spring, Jeffrey began complaining to his parents about a slight pain in his groin area. They waited to see if the symptoms went away on their own. Instead, a small bulge appeared. They rushed him to the doctor to be told their son needed surgery to remove a double hernia. It was due to a congenital disability.

In one week, he was brought to the hospital for surgery. He picked out his favorite stuffed dog to be his companion through the process. And after the surgery and the drugs wore off, he woke up in such immense pain that he asked his mother if his penis had been completely removed.

The recovery was not quick nor easy. He stayed in the hospital for several days. They returned home, where he spent much of his time wrapped up in his bathrobe, lying on the couch. Whatever dark slump surgery had put him in, it was clear he was not quickly outgrowing it. His father noticed a change in him afterward. His bright, bubbly son seemed to have darkened and withdrawn from the world. A vulnerability haunted him like a heavy shadow.

He never appeared to pull out of the emotional slump.

When the family moved to Doylestown, Ohio, after Lionel finished his Ph.D. and landed a job in Akron, Jeffrey suffered. He had to say goodbye to his pet cat, and he was petrified to start school. At Hazel Harvey Elementary, the teacher expressed her concerns about Jeffrey, who had done well listening but struggled to interact with the other children. Even during recess, he did little to engage with the other students. She even wrote on his report card that he appeared to feel neglected.

Winter arrived, and on December 18, 1966, Joyce gave birth to another boy. Joyce's anxiety worsened throughout the pregnancy, but Jeffrey remained excited and hopeful for a little brother to play with. His small hand pressed on his mother's stomach so the baby would know they had a big brother there.

David, who Jeffrey named, was a difficult baby. He cried often and kept the young parents up. Exhausted and overwhelmed, even more of a divide built between them. Joyce's depression worsened, and she returned to spending most of her time bedridden. Lionel took over many of the household chores and watched over the children.

Several months passed, and the family packed up and moved to Barberton. It was another moment of upset in Jeffrey's young life, but his time there began seemingly positively. In Barberton, Jeffrey played outside, running around the yard with his spaniel cross, Frisky, whom he adored.

Though he struggled with social interactions, Jeff became friends with a boy his age named Lee. They often played together, and on Halloween, dressed up as devils to go knocking on neighbor's doors in hopes of getting candy.

There was even a teacher at the school he liked. "I kind of got attached to her, so I thought I'd catch some tadpoles and give them to the teacher as a present. She said thank you and acted like she thought it was a great gift, so that made me happy," Dahmer later recalled. After a few days passed, Jeffrey returned to class to find the tadpole gifts were now gone from the window ledge, where they'd been kept. But Jeffrey later learned that she'd given them away to his friend Lee. This was an act of betrayal. Jeffrey found them swimming in Lee's garage. He took a canister of motor oil and poured it over the tadpoles, killing them.

Ghosts in the Animal Graveyard

In 1968, the family went out for a typical Sunday drive. It was one of the rare times Joyce left the house, and on one particular trip, she fell in love with a home for sale in Bath, Ohio. Almost immediately, they purchased the wood-style, three bedroom ranch. Sitting on 1.5 acres, the house was surrounded by forest for Frisky and Jeff to explore and had a spring-fed pond. Tall trees rose over rolling hills; it was a landscape for Dahmer to escape into, the perfect canvas for his growing fantasies. The family couldn't be happier with the land and space. Here, Jeff helped his father construct a chicken coop and raise sheep and ducks.

At Eastview Junior High School, he made some friends. Bill Henry, Greg Rogerson, and David Borsvold shared a lunch table with him, though most of the students knew him as the quiet, weird kid.

"I was never one to go out and voluntarily play football and baseball or anything like that," he described. "Group sports just didn't interest me." But he and David shared love for geology and the prehistoric era. They spent time together, pedaling on their bikes to one another's home.

And as their relationship grew, Jeffrey built enough trust to reveal a small part of his fantasy world with David. He introduced him to a game that the nine-year-old entitled Infinity Land. He instructed David on the rules: the stickmen would be destroyed if they became too close to one another, as well as spirals that descended into an abyss of nothing. Each had an army of stick men to manage. The bleak game centered around creating distance. It was a game Jeff often played alone, and David was the only one whom he invited in. It was only a sliver of the darkness lurking inside a lonely, distant heart.

At dinner one evening, as the family sat around the table, Dahmer asked his father what would happen to the leftover chicken bones if they were dumped in bleach. To Lionel, it was a question born from sheer curiosity. If anything, the chemist was thrilled by the sudden surge of interest in science taken by his son, and it was a subject he knew well. After supper was finished, Dahmer stood silently beside his father, watching and listening as they laid the chicken bones into a pan of bleach.

Jeffrey was ten years old.

Later, his father gifted him with a basic chemistry set, which he used to experiment with insects and small animals. He and some neighborhood kids played ball or ghost in the graveyard. In the winter, they went sledding down hills in the backyard. Jeff was simply a bit strange to them. He did things the other kids didn't do, like when he caught a fish and took the time to cut it open just to see what was inside. He also liked to press his ear to his friends' chests to listen to their heart beating.

Meanwhile, Joyce's health continued to deteriorate. Fits of shaking consumed her, and no doctor nor specialist could determine the root cause. Her jaw locked tightly, and her back stiffened. She took a daily concoction of laxatives, Equanil, and sleeping pills to get through the day.

To Jeffrey, it grew apparent his mother and father didn't enjoy one another's companionship. He decided he would never get married and never endure the same fate as them. And when their voices filled the house with shouts and screams, he and his younger brother quietly waited until the fighting calmed. There were moments of peace for family hikes through the woods and days spent working together in the garden. Though little fixed the mounting tension between Lionel and Joyce; it finally snapped after a nervous breakdown, and she was taken to the hospital. She remained in a mental ward for two months. Her time in treatment helped, but she never overcame her dependence on pills.

Spending his free time alone in the forest, Jeffrey wandered away from his family, who heard him chopping down trees for firewood. The constant *thwack* of the metal ax against the wood echoed through their property.

Eric Tyson was a few years younger than Jeffrey and was a curious boy. He lived across the street, and the two boys had become friends, spending days in the forest working on a treehouse together or fishing. Jeffrey was around thirteen when they touched and kissed one another, meeting several times in the treehouse to explore these new innocent sexual feelings. They stopped for fear of being caught. There were no emotions of attachment for Jeffrey, but he knew he felt excited about seeing the boy's body. It was his first sexual experience, although innocent.

But during that time, he had developed a new interest. In a small hutch off the road near his home, Jeffrey secluded himself for hours. Here he tended to his animal graveyard full of skeletons he had dissected himself. He preserved insects, soaking them in jars full of formaldehyde. Homemade crosses were stuck into the ground to mark the different forest critters' buried remains, with skulls hanging over them. Most everyone saw it as nothing more than a weird hobby.

One day during biology, Jeff's class was assigned to dissect a baby pig. While most students would be left in shock and disgust, Jeffrey was thrilled. He even asked his teacher if he could keep the baby pig remains and take them home.

When the day was over, he returned to his hutch, where he carefully skinned the head of the baby pig, hanging on to its skull. His father, a fellow chemist, related to his son's interest in science. It was the one thing Jeffery hadn't given up on as he had with tennis or the school newspaper. He was glad there was finally a hobby Jeffrey enjoyed—all else had failed. But unbeknownst to his parents, the interest was manifesting into something deeper that eventually took hold: a profound interest in death. It became an obsession. Jeff remained on alert for roadkill, making sure to stop and bring the creatures back to his hut to dissect properly. None of his experiments died at his hands. He only wished to inspect the dead animals and see what laid beneath their fur, never to kill them.

Puberty and his first sexual encounter began alongside the dissection of animals; some areas of interest started to fuse within Jeffrey. He became aroused not by creating pain, but by the cold, dead, unmoving corpses. His excitement came from peering inside and understanding what caused life— not witnessing the soul in motion, only observing its lifeless vessel.

One particular day, he discovered the body of a beagle in the woods. "I wanted to see what the insides looked like, so I cut it open," he later recalled. After gutting the dog's corpse, he stuck its head onto a pole and left its body hanging. The entrails were draped along the branches of the pine tree. Several local hikers found his display out in the woods and were horrified, snapping a photo.

The ideas of necrophilia began to dance in his head like a slight itch, growing in desperation to be scratched. What was started could not be stopped. While other boys spent time talking about dating or playing sports, Jeffrey's period of sexual development was spent thinking of dissection and biological specimens. He began to wonder what it would be like to cut up a human being. At this early age, his fantasies of being with another man were now interlocked with the fantasies of dismembering a human body.

With no one to talk to and a family breaking before his very eyes, Jeffrey began to drink at sixteen. He was bold about his alcohol consumption and blatantly drank in front of the other students in class. When a classmate asked him what his styrofoam cup of scotch was, he tilted his head back, telling her nonchalantly it was his medicine.

Dressed in an old military jacket, with shaggy hair and large glasses, he was quickly viewed as the weird class clown at Revere High School. He began sporadic episodes of acting ridiculous in hopes of gaining attention. Sometimes in class, he would suddenly bleat like a sheep. Other times he'd pretend to have an epileptic seizure or spit out his food as if he was sick. The other students simply referred to the routine as "doing a Dahmer." He once snuck into the National Honor Society's yearbook photo, even though he wasn't a member. Before the yearbook was printed, his face was blacked out of the picture.

Although he had created a reputation for himself, he still struggled ot maintain friendships with his classmates. The school staff noticed and worried about his apparent aversion to any social behavior. Schoolwork suffered, and his grades dropped off. There was no doubt Jeffrey was an intelligent student, but he had no sense of drive.

His isolation seemed to manifest in his very bones. He stood rigid and stiff. His days were spent alone, planted in front of the television. He latched onto a few hobbies, attempting to participate in soccer, boy scouts, and tennis, only to give them up shortly after starting. His father, along with other around him, continued to worry.

Lionel attempted to pull his son from isolation, but every attempt was met with the same general apathy.

Joyce exhibited similar behavior. She remained tied to her bedroom, transfixed in a self-induced retreat of drugs and sedatives. It was not uncommon for Jeffrey and his brother David to come home after school to find that their mother had not stirred all day.

Mirroring his mother, he began to retreat deeper within himself.

Jeffrey soon was consumed into a pool of darkness and budding sexual fantasy. He made one particular friend around the age of sixteen. Known around the high school for supplying students with marijuana, Jeff Six approached him one day at lunch. He asked if Dahmer wanted to smoke weed. Interested, he agreed and quickly formed a relationship. He was the perfect friend for Jeffrey. Almost every day, he and Six melted away from reality by smoking pot and drinking. A surface-level bond formed between them, allowing them to disconnect from the world. Some semblance of a friendship formed, but Dahmer hated the way Six drove. He later described Six's reckless habit of hitting dogs and how "he'd speed up real fast and just tick them off. The last one was this little puppy that walked into the road, and I remember it was horrible, he speeded up real fast, and the dog just went flipping over the top of the hood, and I looked back, and I could see it running off with this terrified look in its face. I don't know how badly hurt it was, but pretty badly. That just sickened me. I told him to take me back and let me out." If this memory was the last moment of a guilty conscience left in Jeffrey, then it was quickly fading.

Lionel encouraged his son to try bodybuilding. It was the first hobby Jeffrey took to. Many hours were spent at home, Jeffrey in his bedroom and the sound of the rowing machine moving behind the closed bedroom door. But he eventually gave up on it, as he had with everything else.

By seventeen, he had no adult sexual experience beyond his imagination and his innocent encounter in the treehouse. To curb his intense urges, he sometimes masturbated more than three times a day and had managed to collect several gay porn magazines. The fantasies he created were fixated on the beautiful, hairless chests of the men posed nude. That was what aroused Dahmer the most—the idea of the male body for him to control and use as he wished. There was no room for the soul or a relationship. And at some point, between the drinking, the isolation, and the days spent roaming the woods inspecting the animal's innards, the desire to see the inner workings of men's bodies became a necessity.

As his fantasies became increasily darker, Jeffrey began to take notice of a jogger who ran past his house almost every day. The jogger was lean and fit, the type of physique Dahmer fantasized about. He watched as the runner continued along his daily route, perhaps noticing the gleam of sweat on his skin and wondering about the pounding heart in his chest beneath the flesh.

Only weak seams held Jeffrey's inner demons back, and it took little for them to snap. He wanted complete control of the jogger's body for his pleasure—he needed it. Thus, Dahmer devised a plan to obtain what he wanted. He planned to capture the man by knocking him unconscious and then dragging his body through the woods. There they'd be alone, and Dahmer could do with him as he pleased. It would finally be his chance to fulfill his fantasy, to experience his distorted version of intimacy.

Armed with a baseball bat, he decided it was time to act. Anxious, Dahmer stood near the road, concealed within the green shrubbery, excited and full of anticipation for his new type of experiment— much different from the roadkill rotting in the abandoned hut. He lingered, hidden in the woods, waiting.

But a stroke of luck saved the jogger. According to Jeffrey, the jogger didn't run by that day. Defeated, Jeffrey decided to return home. He never pursued the runner again.

By the time Dahmer was a senior in high school, he was a full-fledged alcoholic. It did not help that 1977 was a challenging year for everyone at 4480 West Bath Road. Joyce and Lionel's marriage finally dissolved into a divorce. They had tried counseling, but the final nail in the coffin was when Joyce left in September for her father's funeral. She returned to tell Lionel she had slept with another man on her visit. It wasn't an amicable separation, and a vicious custody battle erupted solely over David, who was only twelve at the time. First, Lionel sued Joyce for "gross neglect of duty and extreme cruelty." She countersued. Exasperated and tired, Lionel decided to move out to live in a motel ten miles down the road while Joyce remained in the house with her two sons.

Completely wrapped up in their fighting and worried about David, who was overtly upset, no one paid Jeffrey much attention. He was eighteen now, and most young men his age would be preparing for college or moving out for the first time. Instead, Jeffrey only became more disconnected from everyone around him. Any discussions of the future and college with his father were met with a blank acceptance. Jeff nodded and agreed, then forgot the conversation. A vast disconnect had formed between them. With Joyce's depression continuing to spiral down along with the marriage, little time or attention was given to Jeffrey. His developing obsession, along with his alcoholism, distracted him from his parents' negligence. He later said: "It was my way of shutting out any painful thoughts, just taking an attitude of not caring or pretending not to care, to save myself the pain of what was going on with the divorce. Maybe it started then. That was effective. It worked."

He turned to the bottle to numb the edge. One teacher found him on school property, sitting on the lawn. He was drunk, surrounded by three empty beer cans as he continued with the twelve pack. The teacher approached Dahmer and told him that he shouldn't be drinking at the school, and that it would have to be reported. Jeffrey made up an excuse on the fly, telling him that he was having problems at home—referring to the divorce—and his counselor was aware. His excuse worked, and the teacher didn't pursue it any further.

When May arrived, it fell upon Dahmer to attend prom. It was a rite of passage, and every American teenager was expected to dance the night away with their date. But he had no candidates or idea of who to take. When it came to talking with girls, Jeffrey was extremely shy. Two classmates, Mike Costlow and Lynn Soquel, took it upon themselves to find Dahmer a date. Though Jeff had no close friends, a small friend group accepted and included him. The day before prom, he approached sixteen-year-old Bridget Geiger. "He came up and said, 'Mike said you'd said you'd go to prom with me, is that right?' That's exactly how he asked me...I knew a week ahead of time, but he was afraid to ask me. He was polite, he did act kind of goofy, but he didn't look like he had a mean bone in his body," Bridget said in a documentary. She was best friends with one of the girlfriends of Jeff's friends, but knew little about him, aside from his drinking and that he was a bit nerdy. What she did know was that he seemed sweet, and he never picked on anyone. If he agreed not to drink, then she would go as his date.

Prom night arrived, and Jeffrey showed up at the Geiger's residence. He knocked on the door wearing dark pants and a bow tie accompanied by a vest instead of the typical tuxedo. Geiger's father opened the door, inspecting the young man who'd be taking his daughter out. When it came to pin the corsages on, Jeffrey was overwhelmed with nerves. His shaking hands moved so slowly that Geiger's mother stepped in to help. He feared the pin might stab her. Neither one of them wanted to take pictures, but Mrs. Geiger insisted, practically dragging the two outside. There Bridget stood beside him, shoulder to shoulder in a long, pretty dress as a few photos were snapped. It was her very first date. He was instructed to bring Bridget back no later than 1:00 a.m., and the two set off for a nice dinner before attending the dance in Akron, Ohio.

They were there for a short while when Bridget realized her date was missing. She thought at first he had gone to the bathroom, but he didn't show up until the very end. Jeffrey explained he had been so nervous during dinner he hadn't eaten, so he went to Mcdonald's to grab a few burgers. Upon returning, he wasn't allowed back into the dance hall. He even kept a few hamburger wrappers to prove his story, apologizing several times to Bridget, but she told him it was fine. She'd made the best of the night and spent time with their friends.

He dropped her off back home after stopping at a bar with a few others. They drank soda and talked. It was around

11:00 p.m. when he left Bridget with nothing more than a handshake, whispering goodnight at her home. The rite of passage proved uneventful and underwhelming for Jeffrey. His interests lied elsewhere.

After graduation, Jeffrey had little structure to help him move forward. He had no real hobbies or the security of his family, only loneliness and his fantasies. Before the divorce was finalized, his father moved out of the house, and his mother often left on long trips. At just eighteen years old, Jeff was living completely alone at 4480 West Bath.

Fantasy Comes True

The jogger had been only the beginning. When Jeffrey masturbated, ideas of complete dominance continually swam through his mind. He wanted ownership through the means of death. While other young men thought of a reciprocating lover with mutual feelings, his thoughts wandered to one-sided control. Something evil brewed beneath the surface, and it appeared the divorce took its toll on him. He later told a probation officer that if there was one thing he could have changed about his childhood, it was that he wished his parents hadn't fought so much. He felt that he had been completely forgotten as they fought desperately for custody over David.

Alone in impending isolation, Jeff masturbated often, and it helped to take off some of the edge. But it proved to be only a temporary fix, like placing a bandaid over a massive gash that only continues to bleed.

Often, he thought about a fantasy of a hitchhiker—a young, well-built man alone and in need of help,someone Jeffrey would pick up and invite back to his home. "I had been having, for a couple of years before that, fantasies of meeting a good-looking hitchhiker and sexually enjoying him," he later revealed.

In mid-June, Jeff was eighteen years old, and his mother took David on one of her extended vacations. Bored, Dahmer reached out to his father, asking if he could borrow the blue Ford. He had no other plans other than catching a movie at the mall. He'd drive his dad back to the motel and return the car the following day. His father agreed.

Behind the wheel, Jeffrey drove down the highway. His eyes scanned the open road. It was early evening, around five o'clock, when the warm summer sun began to descend. He had no prior plans on searching for his first victim; it was only by chance he saw a hitchhiker who was close to his age, around nineteen, standing with his thumb outstretched and shirtless in the evening heat. The man had a bare chest like in all his fantasies. He was handsome as well, with shoulder-length brown hair, wearing blue jeans and a cross necklace. To Jeffrey, it was as if the stars had aligned. He was alone, and there was the ideal man right there in front of him like he'd always craved. He knew he couldn't pass up the opportunity.

He turned the car back nervously and slowed down beside the hitchhiker. Jeffrey explained he had some free time, and they could hang out at his place; drink a few beers and smoke a joint. His parents weren't home. Nineteen-year-old Steven Hicks from Illinois agreed and hopped into the car. There were no visible red flags to the young hitchhiker. Jeffrey was around his age and seemed nice. Steven had just attended a rock concert at Chippewa Lake Park, Ohio, and planned to meet up with friends later that evening. He'd spent the day with them, enjoying the sun and music.

Back at the house, they went into Jeff's room, where he rolled a joint. Hicks turned down the weed but had some beer. Music played through the house, and the conversation came quickly. It appeared to Jeffrey that a real connection was forming between them. Steve was good-looking, and they both were recent graduates from high school. Despite their rapport, Jeffrey grew anxious. His mind spun, crafting different attempts to make a pass at Hicks. He wanted to do something, but Hicks had made it clear he wasn't gay, mentioning he was on his way to visit his girlfriend. But Jeffrey didn't care. He was attracted to Steven and he couldn't stop thinking about how he wanted him to undress. But the fear of being rejected was powerful, and it interrupted the fantasies blooming in Jeffrey's mind. He tried to reassure himself: they were getting along fine, and there was no reason Hicks wouldn't want Jeffrey. Jeffrey wanted him, so he convinced himself Hicks would want him back.

But after several hours passed, Hicks mentioned it was about time he headed out. Rejection, frustration and rage began to rise through Jeffrey. "The guy wanted to leave, and I didn't want him to leave," Jeffrey would confess years later. He couldn't stand another episode of abandonment. Silently, Jeffrey forbade it. He went downstairs and grabbed an eight-inch long barbell without the weights. With his back to the door, Hicks remained unaware of his host while sitting patiently. Jeffrey emerged from the basement like a shadow, ready to claim his prize and win his desire. He raised the barbell and brought it down hard with a heavy strike, hitting Hicks in the back of the head.

Hicks shot up from the seat, confused and in pain, and the two of them began to struggle. Dahmer landed a second quick and devastating blow. Hicks collapsed to the ground, unconscious and still. Without another thought, propelled only by passion and wild drive, Dahmer strangled Hicks to death with the barbell. Now his prize lay before him, never to reject him, never to leave.

He undressed Hicks, running his hands over his bare chest, touching and kissing him. He laid beside him and finally masturbated over the body.

Once the initial thrill subsided, the clarity settled in, followed by the panic. When night came, Jeffrey dragged Hicks out into the front yard then down into the crawl space. He tried to go about his night normally, but he could not sleep as he lay in bed.

His heart boomed in his chest, and his blood pulsed in his ears. He later described that night as a night of panic: "I was out of my mind with fear that night. I didn't know what to do. I had gone to such an extreme." He knew he had to do something—to hide the evidence. 'That night in Ohio, that one impulsive night. Nothing's been normal since then. It taints your whole life," he said. "After it happened, I thought that I'd just try to live as normally as possible and bury it, but things like that don't stay buried. I didn't think it would, but it does; it taints your whole life."

When morning came, he went out to purchase a large knife then returned to the crawl space. In the dark, shallow, empty undergrounds of his home, he dismembered Hicks into pieces. His road kill experiments lent aid to his work as he began by first removing the legs, arms, and then the victim's head. He stuffed the body parts in thick garbage bags, burning all of Steven's clothes and identity cards in barrels fifty yards from the house.

But it wasn't enough.

He knew he couldn't keep the body pieces in the crawl space. The summer heat would wreak havoc on the corpse. Someone could find them, and then what? He panicked and finally came to the solution: at night, he'd dump them in a nearby ravine. No one would ever know it was him. When night came and after he drank enough beer to muster some courage, Jeffery loaded the bags into the blue Ford and drove toward the ravine. It was 3:00 a.m.

He didn't get far. Red and blue lights flashed in the rearview mirror as Dahmer pulled over to the side of the empty country road. A single officer parked behind him and called a second to the scene. They asked Dahmer to step out of the vehicle. He'd been caught driving on the wrong side of the road, and they assumed he was intoxicated. He was brought to the back of the car and asked to perform several sobriety tests. He walked in a straight line and placed his finger on his nose. He passed the tests, but as he finished up, one of the officers shined a flashlight onto the back seat. There the bright light illuminated the plastic bag full of what remained of Steven Hicks. The officer immediately asked what that smell was. Calmly, Dahmer told the officers it was trash. His parents were in the middle of a horrible divorce, he'd explained, and he decided to throw it out late as a means to escape their hostility. Unbelievably, there were no further investigations or questions.

He was written a ticket for erratic driving and sent on his way. Dahmer returned the garbage bags to the crawl space back alone at his house, but he opened one and removed Hicks' severed head. This prize was brought upstairs to his bedroom, and Jeffrey used it to fulfill his disturbing sexual fantasies.

Much like the smell of the rat bones, Jeffrey knew it was only a matter of time before the decaying flesh would attract attention. The next day, he dragged the bags out of the crawl space and stuffed them into a wide drainage pipe on the property, shoveling dirt over it. Unsure of what else to do with the evidence, he threw the knife out into a river. He kept the head in his room until decomposition ran its course and the head began to rot. Jeffrey hoped he'd be able to bury the memories of Hicks and all of the evil things he'd done to him, but he knew, deep down, there was no going back.

First Semester Away

In July 1978, the divorce was finalized. One month later, Joyce loaded up the car and took David to Chippewa Falls. She had relatives there and had no plans to return. She later claimed to have insisted Jeffrey join them, but he didn't want to go.

He was utterly alone once again with nothing but half a gallon of milk in the fridge; that was it. There was no car for him to drive around. He didn't have a summer job. The money lost in the divorce that was originally set aside for his college tuition was now dried up. Graciously, his grandparents offered to pay for him to attend Ohio State University. He apathetically thanked them. He hung around several friends, including Jeff Six. They smoked weed and drank, but they had no emotional connection with Jeffery. Even after four years of high school, he had no one who he was actually close to.

That summer, he invited several friends over, including Bridget Geiger and Mike Costlow. It was a typical gathering. Bridget described that there was "no music, no food, no drinks– it was a nerd party. There were seven people at the whole thing. Then, after we sat down and were situated, the lights went out and one of the kids – not Dahmer – said, 'Let's call Lucifer.' Then, the flame on the candles snapped." A good Catholic girl, Bridget bolted out of the house at the sight of it all, frightened. It was the last time she'd ever see Jeffrey until his photo was plastered across almost every television in America.

Away, Lionel called now and then to check in with his sons. He spoke with David often as well as Jeff. But in August, the calls dropped off. For a week, he attempted to contact the house every day, and every one of those calls was left unanswered. Concern crept in. After receiving permission from the court, he got into his car and drove by. Joyce's car was nowhere to be found, so Lionel decided he had to check in.

Shari Jordan, Lionel's new girlfriend, waited in the passenger seat as they drove to 4480 West Bath Road. Lionel knocked on the front door, waiting. It took a moment, but finally, it creaked open.

"Where's your mother?" Lionel demanded his oldest son. Jeffrey didn't answer, even when questioned about his brother. Over his son's shoulder, Lionel saw other people inside, other teenagers hanging around the house. He instructed all the friends to leave then began interrogating his son about Joyce. Before leaving, she ordered Jeffrey not to tell his father she'd moved. It took a moment, but finally, Jeffrey admitted that his mother and David were gone and had relocated.

"Moved where?" Lionel pried.

"I don't know." Jeff shrugged. Shari wandered in then, taken aback by the messy state of the home as well as the scared and confused young man before her. She pitied Jeffrey. She found a pentagram drawn with chalk on the coffee table and discovered the fridge didn't even work.

Seeing the home in its state, Lionel decided Jeffrey shouldn't be alone. He and Shari moved in almost immediately. At first, the move went well. Jeffrey was pleasant, perhaps relieved his stretch of loneliness had ended. The house was cleaned up, and there were groceries and warm homemade dinners now. Maybe, if they'd found Jeffrey months prior, some part of him could have been saved. But it was too late now.

The pleasantness quickly declined. One afternoon when Shari stopped by the house on the way to a doctor's appointment, the stench of alcohol hit her like a wall. She followed it to Jeff's bedroom to find him passed out on his bed. His sentences came out in broken slurs as he pulled himself upright.

"I had a few friends over," he said. He explained that they'd had a few drinks. But few was quite the understatement. Jeffrey had consumed almost half a fifth of Jack Daniels. Shari immediately called Lionel to come home, telling him that his son was close to blacking out. In frustration and disbelief, his father lectured and chastised him. But Dahmer heard little and seemed to care even less. He told his father he only drank because he was bored. That was it.

Reflecting on recent events in his life, getting too drunk was nothing compared to what he had done to Steven Hicks. How trivial it all must have seemed to Jeffrey. It makes complete sense he would shrug off getting caught knee-deep in a liquor bottle.

Later Shari's rings and jewelry disappeared. Lionel was certain it was one of Jeff's friends, who had been over often drinking and hanging around. One day, they sat Jeff down to speak with him about the stolen jewelry, but he was insulted by the accusation made against his buddy and got up to leave the room. Shari, a confident and direct woman, rose from her chair and demanded Jeff return to his seat. It was then she saw a side to Jeffrey she hadn't seen before. She later told Lionel she witnessed "a flash of terrible rage" within Jeffrey's eyes. As quickly as it arrived, it subsided, his face returning to a dull, blank expression.

He remained in his room after his father banished his small friend group. The summer dwindled.

Shari took it upon herself to help prepare Jeff for college. The fall semester was fast approaching, and he was about to attend his first semester at Ohio State University. She took him shopping for a new wardrobe, chatting about how fun and exciting college is. Jeffrey could not match her excitement. The only important additions he could think to put in his luggage were two snake skins and a photo of his dog, Frisky.

In September of 1978, Shari and Lionel drove Jeffrey to campus to begin his education. But even though Shari had done her best to encourage him, Jeffrey arrived with little eagerness.

He was moved into Ross House dormitory, Room 541, and had three male roommates, all of whom found Dahmer to be a bit odd. He spent most of his time in the top bunk listening to a Beatles album on repeat. He stuck a photo of Vice President Walter Mondale to the wall. But what was most upsetting was the amount of liquor Dahmer consumed; it was not uncommon for him to down multiple whiskey bottles a day. And to accommodate the expensive drinking, he donated blood two times a week at the plasma center. Eventually, the center had him marked, preventing him from donating more than once a week. He made no effort to make new friends or attend any lectures, and became nothing more than a drunken puddle melting into the sheets of his bed. His roommates, though concerned, found it best to leave Jeff alone.

His behavior was erratic and volatile. One evening when the three roommates headed off to a party, Dahmer was left alone. A swirl of emotions overtook him. He stacked all the furniture into piles and, in a fit, hurled slices of pizza onto the walls. When they returned to the mess, he provided no explanation for his fit. He'd kicked the tile off the wall and caused property damage. His destructive behavior was not limited to vandalizing the dorm. When the guys were away at lectures, Jeffrey stole from them and pawned off their items for cash to buy more booze. The fall after Steven Hicks, it was clear that all Jeff knew to do was drink.

He fooled his father and Shari when they came to visit. Proudly, he showed off his clean and neat room. Later on a second visit, he walked around campus with them, and to his father, Jeff appeared genuinely happy.

But reality came crashing down when Lionel received Jeffrey's first-quarter grades in the mail. He opened the envelope to find that Jeff had achieved a lowly .45 GPA. He had accumulated only two credit hours and was promptly removed from school. Shari and Lionel drove back to Columbus to collect Jeffrey.

Lionel spoke with Jeffrey's roommate. They told him about his son's severe drinking problem. Lionel learned how Jeff would start drinking early until he passed out in the evening, and when he woke up in the mornings, he was incapable of moving, laying in the top bunk, only to start drinking again.

Lionel and Shari brought the college dropout back home. Unfortunately, Jeffrey's situation did not improve. Shortly after returning, he disappeared into a cloud of marijuana with his buddy Jeff Six. On several occasions, he borrowed Lionel's car only to return home and admit he couldn't remember where he parked. Upset, Shari and Lionel had no choice but to go out and find it.

His behavior was reaching a breaking point. Lionel presented Jeff with two options: either he got a job or joined the armed forces. For a few weeks, Lionel drove his son to Summit Mall, dropped him off to job hunt then arrived in the early evening to pick him up. Sometimes, Jeff was fine, almost normal. But other days, the drunken glaze was visible in his blue eyes. He'd wasted hours drinking and stumbling through the mall.

One particular evening, Jeffrey came out to the parking lot to greet his father, blatantly intoxicated. Furious, Lionel told him before returning home, Jeff had to stay and sober up. The understandably upset father drove away, unwilling to put Shari, now his wife, through any more of Jeffrey's antics. But the evening grew late, and the mall closed. Jeffrey never called. Lionel drove back to the mall around ten o'clock to an empty parking lot with his son was nowhere in sight. After a few calls, he discovered the police had picked Jeffrey up; he'd been arrested for drunken disorderly conduct. Lionel bailed him out.

Shame shrouded Jeffrey as he silently sat in the car. And upon returning home, he apologized to his father and stepmother, then shuffled to his bedroom. His door closed, he removed himself from the world outside.

In the morning, it became clear Jeffrey had lost all other options but to enlist. Lionel drove him to the recruiting office, where an interview date was set and paperwork filled out. By the end of January, he was out of the house, headed down to Alabama to begin basic training.

The first four weeks were rigorous. No alcohol was permitted, and for being overweight, he was placed on a diet of five hard-boiled eggs a day. Duties and activities kept Dahmer focused. There was no free time to let the memories of Steven Hicks' murder haunt him or for the fantasies to dance in his mind. But as soon as drinking was allowed, he quickly returned to the habit. Often, he received punishment for being drunk. On one occasion, though, his platoon found him drunk and incompetent. It was time they punished him, and it was not a light slap on the wrist. They beat Jeff severely, gathered around him, kicking hard and punching as he curled up on the floor. During this attack, Jeffrey's eardrum ruptured, and for the next ten years, he suffered from earaches.

On May 11, 1978, Jeffrey moved to the Army Hospital School in San Antonio, Texas, beginning courses to become a medic. This time he did well in his studies. Things seemed to be heading in a positive direction for once. After the six-week course ended, he was a qualified medic. Medic students are taught a vast amount about the human body. Jeffrey saw this as information to use later, but never to save a life.

With training finished, his father waited at the bus station. Jeffery stepped off in phenomenal shape and with a great, beaming smile. His father stood in shock. It was almost a miracle to see Jeff this happy and in shape. Back at home, he helped around the house, chopping wood and raking leaves. They'd cook outside on the grill and play tennis. For two weeks, the family saw a brief glimpse of a happy Jeffrey. He was someone with goals and direction now, and Jeffrey's improved state allowed the father and son to spend quality time together and bond. Lionel nearly convinced himself that the darkness and dullness in Jeffrey were gone now. But it was only an illusion, for there on the hill several yards away, Steven Hicks body remained stuffed in the drainpipe, waiting in silence to be discovered.

Number 2/68 Armour Division

In June 1979, Dahmer said goodbye to his father after his brief visit home. He had been assigned to Number 2/68 Armour Division, Second Battalion, and stationed in Baumholder, West Germany.

For the two years he served in Germany as a medic, he was known among the other soldiers as a loner. Though they noticed he was an intelligent guy, it was clear he had no ambitions, and the alcoholism was blatant. With alcohol banned in the barracks, Private First Class Dahmer, Jeffrey L., fashioned himself a minibar out of a suitcase. When the suitcase snapped open, he gained access to a martini shaker, stirrers, and liquor. He listened to Black Sabbath in his free time, pulling the headphones tight over his ears, lounging atop his bunk. He blasted the heavy metal to shut out the world and drank from his makeshift minibar until he passed out. On some weekends, Jeffrey would disappear without a word about where he was headed, often returning a day late.

After finding out he'd never kissed a woman, the men dragged him out to the popular brothel in Vogelweh,

Annabella's House. There he was introduced to a girl, but when his mates parted ways, Dahmer slipped out unnoticed without doing anything sexual. His friends wrote it off as nothing more than his shyness, though one noticed how "he always seemed like he was hiding something." He purchased gay pornography to offer some relief.

Jeff's free time was spent alone walking along the roads of the countryside or shooting guns. He recalled, "I fired M-60s in the army...Those things will go through three inches of solid steel. And I fired 45s."

He wrote little letters to his father. Shari made sure to send him many pictures of the home and garden. Jeffrey called his parents several times, and to his father, he appeared to be happy—albeit sometimes short and withdrawn. Lionel assumed that was simply caused by exhaustion. His father thought the army had created a new Jeff, one with purpose and a future ahead of himself. Despite the frequent calls, Jeffrey never mentioned his family to the other soldiers.

He was quiet and reserved unless his drinking turned volatile. Racial slurs and shouts left his mouth. He became angry, and those blue eyes twisted like a brewing storm.

In an interview, Jeffrey told investigators it was in Germany when he was first approached about sleeping with another man. He was working at Lansthole Hospital at the time, out drinking later in the evening. One of the Sergeants found him at the Local NCO club. In a friendly way, he approached Jeff and mentioned there was a party back at his apartment, inviting him. But when they arrived, there was no one else present. The sergeant filled a bowl full of hash, taking a few hits, and offered it to Dahmer, who accepted. Beers were had, and the sergeant slipped into the shower. When he got out, he went to bed and tried to coax Jeffrey in with him.

"No, thanks," Jeffrey said, dazed from the marijuana and alcohol. He then staggered out of the apartment.

But this was not his only encounter. Preston Davis was twenty years old when he met Jeffrey while serving in Germany. They were both assigned to work in the medic unit. "I was raped by Jeffrey," Davis later said. "I am just thankful to be alive to tell the story."

Davis had eight months left in Germany when Dahmer arrived. He saw how Dahmer drank excessively, drowning in booze. "He became a monster once he started drinking," Davis recalled in an interview. "Alcohol is what turned him into a monster." He transformed from a reserved, quiet man into a loud, outwardly racist bigot, annoying the other soldiers. He described, "Jeffrey had killed his first victim a year before joining the military, and he would get drunk in the barracks and say, 'I killed the guy in Ohio,' and we'd say, 'you didn't kill nobody!'"

And in October of 1979, Davis and Jeffrey were together working on a field exercise in Belgium. Their vehicle broke down, so it had to be towed to a train station. Somewhere in the mix of it all, Davis says it was then Dahmer drugged and assaulted him. "The reason he didn't kill me—he said after I left, 'I should've killed that n—r when I had the chance' —but that was the reason he couldn't kill me: We were out in the middle of Belgium. He had no idea how to get back to Germany."

After Preston Davis left, Billy Joe Capshaw arrived in Germany at the age of seventeen. At first, Capshaw thought his new roommate was overall a likable person, but immediately, he grew terrified of his bunkmate. It didn't take long for Dahmer to lose control. He drank and then beat Billy Capshaw, who came forward to superiors and told them what Dahmer was doing. They wrote him off and called him a "pussy." The abuse only worsened as Jeffrey's inner turmoil grew. He used an iron bar from one of the beds to hit Capshaw's joints on multiple occasions. Unable to take anymore, Billy once escaped through the window down the fire escape but had nowhere to stay aside from a hotel for several nights. And when he returned, Dahmer beat him as punishment for leaving.

When Dahmer drugged him or choked him unconscious, Capshaw would wake up tied to the bed, and then Dahmer would rape him. The shame and guilt were overwhelming. "I thought about killing him, and I thought about killing myself," Capshaw confessed. Every request for a room transfer was ignored. "I had probably been raped 8 to 10 times. I don't know. He was tying me to the bunk with motor-pool rope. He took all my clothing from me. He would either beat me before he raped me, or he would beat me after."

Capshaw was eventually brought to the dispensary for a rape kit test, but the doctors did nothing. Even more troubling news came out later. He found out the kit had been thrown out. "I was there for another 17 months with Jeff, being raped and tortured by him."

But things were different according to Jeffrey. He claimed that he laid low during his time in Germany. He claimed there "just wasn't an opportunity to fully express what I wanted to do. There was just not the physical opportunity to do it then." Despite the horrific events alleged against him, he never admitted to the police what he'd done to those two young men.

Years later, when the news of his killings broke out, several investigators in Germany attempted to link him to five unsolved murders. His name was cleared from the list since all the victims had been women.

His constant drinking and complete lack of duty eventually caught up to him. After two years, two months, and fifteen days, he was to reenter the world as a civilian. His drinking and outbursts couldn't be tolerated anymore. He was given an honorable discharge, and left the service as a failed, drunken medic who once told a commanding officer the sight of blood made him uneasy.

As he packed his bags and said farewell to his bunkmates, he joked with them, saying, "Someday you'll hear about me again."

His squad leader, David G. Gross, drove Jeffrey to the airport for his flight back to America. They chatted with one another, but Gross sensed something dark and haunting about Jeff. He recounted their drive, "There was something bugging him in Germany. I knew he had a troubled past, and I knew he had something gnawing at him. He'd say there was something he could not talk about."

Sunshine and Sandwiches

Three months before his military service came to an end, Lionel opened the front door of his home to discover Jeffrey's trunk sitting at the doorstep. He opened it. Folded neatly inside were Jeffrey's army fatigues, jacket, and trousers, but no note or any sign of where his son was. Jeffrey had landed in South Carolina from Germany on March 26, 1981. After he went through processing, Jeff was told they'd provide a ticket for anywhere in the United States. He chose Miami, Florida.

He feared returning home to Shari and Lionel. The shame of being let go early was too much. The Florida heat and sun seemed like a good plan; he flew to Miami and grabbed a hotel room along Collins Avenue with an ocean view. He stayed there for a week until the money ran out. Then, for a month, he lived beneath the green leaves of mangroves, showering once or twice a week inside a hotel.

After living in the Miami sun for two months, he landed a job at Sunshine Subs, a local sandwich shop. He claimed to have worked long hours from morning to night, seven days a week with the occasional day off. However, some coworkers noticed how he missed shifts and was too drunk to work some days, leaving early. But Jeffrey told officers with those long hours that there was little time for recreation. What money he did make, he quickly spent on liquor and drinks.

Jeffrey eventually befriended one of the other workers, a twenty-eight-year-old English woman desperate to solidify her stay in America, for she had no green card. They often spoke, and she even asked Jeffrey if he would marry her to become a citizen. Despite their friendship, he had little interest in helping her and declined the proposal.

Jeff continued to spend his nights alone, and he hated sleeping on the beach. To cope with the burden of homelessness, he drank in excess, staying up well into the early hours of the morning, drinking, before returning to his spot.

But it quickly became clear to him that this lifestyle couldn't be maintained. It was obvious to Jeffrey his time in Miami was coming to a close. He finally decided to call his father and ask about returning home.

Dahmer's time in Florida seemed to be weeks of drinking, wandering, and drinking some more. Overall, an uneventful time with no violence, only alcohol.

But later, when Jeffrey Dahmer was arrested, he was asked if he kidnapped six-year-old Adam Walsh from Sears in 1981. Dahmer was adamant he had nothing to do with the case.

July 27, 1981, Adam Walsh and his mother visited Sears at the shopping mall in Hollywood, Florida, only minutes from Sunshine Subs. When Revé Walsh's six-year-old son asked if he could watch some of the older kids play video games in the toy section, she consented and left him to continue with her shopping. She was not gone for more than ten minutes but returned only to find her son was missing. The store clerk called out his name on the sound system. Then the police arrived on the scene, still no sign of Adam.

A month and a half later, on August 10, 1981, Adam Walsh's head was discovered in a drainage pipe in Verona Beach, Florida, almost one hundred miles away from Hollywood, Florida, by two fishermen. His body has never been found, and to this day, his death remains a mystery.

Although, in December 2008, Chief Chadwick Wagner held a press conference announcing he believed deceased drifter Ottis Toole was the perpetrator. There was never enough evidence to prosecute, and multiple times, Toole redacted his confession, claiming it wasn't him. He could not properly identify Adam Walsh nor describe his appearance. He was notorious for admitting to murders he never committed.

On the day Walsh was kidnapped, two witnesses called the police and described seeing a man near the location of the kidnapping with blond hair who exhibited bizarre behavior and looked disheveled. Through his work, Jeffrey also had access to a blue van that fit the getaway vehicle's. The owner's two restaurants used the vans as delivery cars, and all the employees could take the keys at will. There was no system to keep track.

One of the many witnesses who believed to have seen Jeffrey Dahmer at the mall that day was Bill Bowen, an Alabama TV producer. He saw a man struggling to put a child into the back of a blue van illegally parked in the Sears parking lot. Bowen claimed the boy shouted, "I'm not going. I don't want to go!" The two struggled. "Yes, you are," the man screamed, with his hand wrapped around the boy's arm, before tossing him in and speeding away.

And when the news came out in 1991 about Dahmer and his crimes, his photo plastered across the media, more witnesses called into the Hollywood police believing there was a significant connection. They had seen Jeffrey at the mall the day Adam Walsh went missing.

FBI agent Neil Purtell believed Dahmer inadvertently admitted to killing Adam Walsh with his fervent denials. "Honest to God, Neil, I didn't do it." Then Dahmer's words chilled Purtell. He said, 'You know, Neil, anyone who killed Adam Walsh could not live in any prison, ever." Many speculate that Dahmer couldn't confess that he killed Adam Walsh for the sole reason that being a pedophile would get him killed in prison.

Time with Grandma

"Sorry, Dad. I guess I had a few too many on the plane." Disheveled and filthy, Jeffrey stumbled out of the plane at the Cleveland airport and into his father's car, drunk. His mustache had grown wild, and stains covered his clothes. He stank horribly of cigarettes and alcohol.

At home, he worked around the house, helping where he could. Winter came, and he quickly volunteered to wrap the drainage pipes down in the crawl space, insistent. He was the one who did it, emerging with a smile as his father watched, unaware of what had occurred several years before down below the foundation.

And when the house was empty, and he had some time, Jeffrey returned to the drainage pipe. There he removed the bags of Steven Hicks, who had remained for years, a still, sleeping shadow of nightmarish memories. All the flesh was now gone, and only the bones remained. In his hand, Jeffrey grasped a massive rock and began smashing the remains into dust, bit by bit. When his victim's remains were splintered into tiny fragments, he gathered the remnants, and went into the woods, spreading Steven Hicks across the forest like dust.

Jeffrey's drinking never stopped. His father dropped him off at Summit Mall to job hunt. Although his family wanted him to be responsible, he couldn't resist falling into his bad habits. It only took two weeks for the twenty-one-year-old to be arrested for drunken disorderly behavior at the Ramada Inn. Several times, he lost track of where he'd left the car, or he'd return home without his glasses or wallet, unable to recollect the evening's events. Lionel and Shari were at their wit's end with Jeff. The army had failed, they couldn't leave him at the house alone anymore, and he had proven incapable of finding a job on his own.

"He roamed around the bars and repeatedly stayed until closing time, and then he would demand more drinks," Lionel told reporters. "They'd usher him out. Sometimes there'd be fights. He'd get hurt badly. He was attacked several times and had stitches over his eye and broken ribs."

They decided it would be best to send him to Grandmother's home in a suburb near Milwaukee.

By the winter of 1981, Jeffrey hugged his father once again at the bus station. His eyes remained fixed, unwavering, in their constant passive state. Little emotion passed between them, and he began his journey to West Allis, Wisconsin.

He arrived at 2357 South 57th Street, a quiet subdivision only a quick drive to the city. His grandmother lived in a two-story home, with a side entrance to the basement, giving Jeffrey privacy to come and go.

Lionel's mother, Catherine Dahmer, now a widow, was growing lonely, and for a bit of work around the house and garden, she'd happily provide Jeffrey room and board. It was an agreeable arrangement right away. Jeffrey loved his grandmother, once describing her in an interview, "I guess she's what you could call a perfect grandmother...very kind, goes to church every Sunday, easy to get along with, very supportive, loving, just a very sweet lady."

On the surface, his time with his grandmother unfolded wonderfully. Jeffrey spent time mowing the lawn or shoveling the heavy snowfall during winter. He helped with the flower bed in the garden and ran errands. She'd cook and wash his laundry, enjoying the company of her grandson, whom she loved dearly, showering him with love and affection. From the outside, everything seemed normal.

He started a job drawing blood at the Milwaukee Blood Plasma Center. His first summer was uneventful. Once again, his family believed there was a chance Jeffrey might create an everyday, normal life for himself. But his father's hope rested on shaking ground, for the evil in Jeffrey had not disappeared. The little progress he made would, in time, become part of the cycle he was trapped in until he completely fell apart.

In the chilly month of January 1982, Jeff purchased a .357 snub-nose Magnum. He claimed it was only used for target practice, but when his grandmother found it, she was disturbed and called his father. They made him hand it over. As passive as always, Jeffrey did not hesitate or protest.

But there were other secrets kept, like black ink slowly bleeding to the surface of his mind. He obtained a copy of Anton LaVey's *Satanic Bible*. And while at the plasma bank, he claimed his curiosity took over. Dahmer admitted to stealing a vile of human blood, slipping into his pocket until he was alone on the roof. He pressed the glass to his lips and took several sips. The irony taste rested on his tongue, but he immediately spit out the blood. He thought the taste was awful.

Summer rolled around, and on August 7, 1982, the Milwaukee State Fair came to town. Families and children gathered at the fairground to enjoy the day's activities. Jeffrey also attended in a drunken cloud. He staggered forward and pushed his pants down to his ankles, followed by his underwear. Families looked upon in horror and confusion. This was the first account of him exposing himself. The police hurried to the messy scene, and he was arrested for disorderly conduct. The officer "observed the defendant with his pants pulled down and his penis exposed leaning against the planter on the south side of the Coliseum in which 25 people were present including women and children." Upon being arrested, he gave his father's address, worried about the shame and repercussions of his actions finding Grandmother Catherine. On his record, the arrest was for public urination.

This event signified the beginning of another downward spiral. Soon after his arrest, he lost his job drawing blood after only ten months. He was fired for poor performance.

Thanksgiving came. Jeffrey drove with Catherine back to Bath, Ohio. Something inspired Dahmer to do better. With the help of his grandmother, he wanted to live an upstanding life. He feared bringing his dear grandmother any more embarrassment.

For a time, it looked like he might have completely turned his life around. He began to attend service with Catherine on Sundays and read the Bible with her. "I was reading the Bible then, trying to get my life straightened around, and I'd give some money to the street people sometimes or send it into different missionaries," he recalled. The support of the church and his grandmother helped him for two years. He said he repressed any desire to sleep with men and masturbated only once a day. It was two whole years in which Jeffrey did not fall into temptation of any kind. He even visited his mother for the first time since the divorce. Christmas of 1983 was spent with David and Joyce. It was the last time Jeffrey would see his mother until one year before his arrest in 1991.

In a store's window, a male mannequin displayed new fashion. Jeffrey noticed the figure while walking down the street through Southridge. He decided he wanted it to take home and use it for sex. He entered the store, hiding until close, and waited until just before midnight. Jeffrey moved quickly in the shadow of the dark empty store, undressing the mannequin, and slipped a sleeping bag over the top of it before sneaking out. "I ended up getting a taxi and brought it back and kept it with me a couple of weeks," he later explained. "I just went through various sexual fantasies with it, pretending it was a real person, pretending that I was having sex with it, masturbating, and undressing it."

In the basement, the makeshift sex doll helped ease his intense fantasies, but his grandmother eventually came across it while cleaning. In Jeff's room, she found the stiff mannequin standing in his closet fully dressed. When she asked Jeff about it, he gave her a weak excuse, telling her it was a prank. Like the gun, Catherine called her son and daughter-in-law, expressing concern. And Lionel immediately questioned Jeff, who told his father he did it to see if he could. Again, it was a joke. Lionel accepted the reason but demanded he return it, but it was too late. Jeffrey had already thrown it away, pulling it apart and smashing it into the trash.

It was this year when David Dahmer made a trip to visit with his older brother and Grandmother. He was eighteen and planned to stay for several nights, sleeping beside Jeffrey. Night came, and they got into bed. Laying in the dark, the wanting consumed Jeffrey. Inches from him was another man, still and unconscious. It didn't seem to matter to Jeffrey that this man was his own brother. Jeffrey reached out a hand beneath the blankets and attempted to touch his younger brother. Immediately, David put a stop to it, leaving an Jeffrey embarrassed and apologetic. He did not attempt to touch his brother again.

In mid-January of 1985, Jeffrey began working six days a week from 11 p.m. to 7 a.m. at Fifth Street and Highland Avenue. Located right in downtown Milwaukee, the Ambrosia Chocolate Factory hired Jeffrey Dahmer as a mixer, paying him around nine dollars an hour. It was a steady paycheck in, and the overnight shift of 11:00 p.m. until 7:30 a.m. came with fewer supervisors and little social interaction.

It was another turn toward living a typical life, but he became more aware of his sexuality and his attraction to men during this time. Jeffrey was smack-dab in the middle of his twenties and settling into adulthood. He later revealed that there was one specific encounter that intensely churned his anger and need for sexual gratification with a person.

A stranger passed him as he sat reading in the West Allis public library. A folded piece of paper landed in his lap. Carefully, he opened it to read:

Meet me in the second-level bathroom. I'll give you a blow job.

He reread the note several times in disbelief, his heart pounding. Though Jeff did not pursue the invitation or interact with the man who passed him the note, the incident began to unravel those dark fantasies and thoughts he had tried to lock away. Jeffrey turned to obsessive masturbation for release, but it wasn't enough.

The note was a catalyst for Jeff to slip back into his old habits. He stopped attending church with his Grandma, and he began drinking in excess.

He wanted to find a partner solely for sexual gratification. He paid visits to adult stores specializing in gay porn. Later in an interview, Dahmer confessed to spending thousands over the years on pornographic material. In these shops, he discovered the coin-operated video booth's door; when left ajar, it was an invitation for a second person to join. Or other shops had "back rooms" where men gathered in complete darkness to give in to any sexual desire with complete anonymity. No conversations were had, no names shared.

His curiosity led him to the bathhouses, and he quickly became a constant figure in the Milwaukee gay scene as a quiet loner. He began to frequent Club Bath Milwaukee. The club had amenities such as coffee bars and television lounges. Saunas with pools and jacuzzis were a frequent hub for men to walk around in nothing but a towel. Usually, on the upper levels, makeshift cubicles with beds were reserved for hookups. Jeff began to indulge in sleeping with men at the bathhouse, learning what he wanted. He found he did not like to receive anal sex and was put off if his partner asked for too much. "I looked at it as an experience of taking," Jeffrey explained. 'There wasn't any mutual giving, not in my mind anyway. I was always quite selfish." Quickly, he discovered he desired a partner to lay completely still and accept whatever Jeffrey wanted with no objection and no movement. In Jeffrey's mind, these people were simply objects for him to use; he was not interested in their feelings or experiences at all.

During a visit to the doctor on June 6, 1986, Jeffrey explained the strange hours of working night shifts affected his sleep, and his body was suffering from these unnatural hours. It was a lie. But it worked, and unknowingly, the doctor wrote him a prescription for sleeping pills he would go on to use on his victims.

With sleeping pills and liquor tucked away, Jeffrey returned to the bathhouse. In the privacy of the cubicle, he slipped the drugs into the unsuspecting victim's drink, and within minutes, he had an unconscious body to play with. Over time, he experimented with his victims to find out the required amount of sleeping pills to keep them unconscious. Too little, and they may wake up or never fall asleep. Too much and they'd become sick. Some of the men noticed he was far more focused on them taking the drink than the actual sex. In time, he learned that five pills was the ideal dose.

He managed to drug and assault several men with no repercussions. A few reported minor complaints to

71

management, but there was no punishment until he put a man into such a deep sleep, he did not wake up. The bathhouse staff took the man to a hospital, where he woke up two days later. The authorities were not involved out of fear of it affecting business at the bathhouse. The staff took away his membership and told Jeffrey he could never return.

This didn't stop Jeffrey. He replaced the bathhouse with an inexpensive room at the Ambassador Hotel. On six different occasions, Jeffrey brought men back to the hotel and drugged them. He struggled to have an erection when they were awake and waited until they fell asleep. Then he'd masturbate over them three or four times, laying beside them, stroking their skin. In his mind, they belonged to him completely. In their unconscious state, they were powerless, and they couldn't reject him or leave him. Often he'd press his ear to their chests and listen to their hearts or their organs. The men woke confused with hours of their night missing and no explanation, utterly unaware of what dark desires Jeffrey subjected their bodies to.

He had a strategy for hunting men: he found them at the bars. There he'd sit at a table drinking or smoking by himself, engaging in little conversation. Others around him packed in to dance beneath the bright flashing lights and thumping music, but for Jeffrey, it was a chance to find a new possession to entrap and take home. His grandmother hated how he'd come in late at night, but Jeffrey did little to soothe her worries. He paid rent now and was heading down a his twisted path; he did not want to stop. He masturbated more and more, purchasing large amounts of pornographic material. The fantasies grew until they were almost tangible, nearly real to Jeffrey. He knew how to make it come true. He wanted a man, lean and fit, but hairless and attractive. He wanted a man to belong to him.

He attended the funeral of an eighteen-year-old after skimming through the obituary columns. The young man was a suitable candidate for Jeffrey's needs, so he waited and watched to see where the teenager was buried. When night came, he returned, intending to dig the body up and bring it to his grandmother's basement. With a shovel in hand, Jeff began to shovel but stopped. The cold Wisconsin ground was too frozen to yield to his carnal desires. He returned home empty-handed.

September 8, 1986, near the Kinnickinnic River Parkway, two twelve-year-old boys saw Jeffrey standing with his pants pulled down and his shirt up. According to Jeff, "I was drinking some beer in an undeveloped wooded area alone. After a few cans of beer, I needed to go, so I did, behind some trees. I was sure there was no one else around, but I was wrong. Two boys saw me and called the police."

But what the boys saw was different. On the grassy hill, they saw a man who appeared to be pleasuring himself.

"Are you having fun?" one shouted.

"'Yeah, I'm having a great time," Jeffrey yelled back. The boys went to the police, who picked up Jeffrey Dahmer and charged him. He had exposed himself in public five times before that day.

The judge put him on one-year probation, but a part of his sentencing was to undergo a psychological evaluation and therapy. He struggled through both of them, rigid and going to extreme lengths to avoid any self-reflection. His therapist Evelyn Rosen's prognosis, written in her notes, stated, "...no doubt at this time that he is a Schizoid Personality Disorder who may show marked paranoid tendencies. He is definitely

SPOOKY!" Clinician Kathy Boese wrote in her concluding report that Jeffrey "...could become a psychopathic deviate (sociopath) with schizoid tendencies. His deviant behavior will at least continue in some form if not be exacerbated . . . Without some type of intervention which is supportive, his defenses will probably be inadequate, and he could gravitate toward further substance abuse with possible subsequent increased masochism or sadistic tendencies and behaviors."

On September 9, 1987, Jeffrey Dahmer arrived at the probation office to fill out his monthly report. Less than a week later, Jeffrey would kill for the second time.

Torn to Shreds

Catherine Dahmer was unaware of the nightmares occurring in her basement. It would be hard for her—or anyone—to conjure such dark ideas about her grandson, even when she crept down the stairs one night to find Jeffry with another young man who appeared drunk. She watched as the man suddenly fell and hit his head; she quickly retreated upstairs, confused and unsure what her grandson was up to. It was only a tiny glimpse of the absolute horror.

Steve Tuomi visited Club 219 after leaving work in mid-September of 1987. The sandy-haired and bright smiling twenty-five-year-old came from the tiny town of Ontonagon, Michigan. After graduating high school, he headed to the city, where he eventually worked as a short-order cook at a diner, flipping burgers on the grill. He had the overnight shift, usually heading home after 6 a.m. But the night of the 21st, he headed down to Club 219.

When the night came to a close and the bars began to shut down, crowds of people pooled in the streets, grabbing taxis and planning rides home. It was then when Jeffrey caught sight of the handsome Tuomi, and the two casually struck up a conversation. Dahmer found out Tuomi had no plans for the rest of the night and invited him over to the Ambassador hotel. Tuomi accepted.

Back at the seedy hotel in an area where many sex workers roamed, Jeffrey opened the door to his hotel room. He made them each a rum and coke. The night heated up as they undressed and climbed into bed together. At some point, Jeffrey slipped in a mix of sleeping pills and liquor in Tuomi's drink. He'd been planning on using it on someone at the club that night. They kissed and pleasured each other, cuddling until the sleeping pills took their toll and Tuomi drifted away. Jeffrey continued to stroke and touched his new victim, but at some point, Jeffrey snapped. "It's almost like I temporarily lost control of myself," he said. "I don't know what was going through my mind. I have no memory of it. I tried to dredge it up, but I have no memory of it whatsoever."

In the morning light, Jeffrey Dahmer awoke. His head pounded as he slowly opened his eyes. Then the realization came- he was atop of a dead body. Steve Tuomi's head hung over the edge of the bed. Red blood ran out of the corner of his mouth, dripping onto the floor. The sharp point of a rib cage poked into him. Jeffrey took in his disturbing work. "I felt complete shock," he recalled. "Just couldn't believe it. Shock, horror, panic, I just couldn't believe it happened again after all those years when I'd done nothing like this." He'd savagely beaten Tuomi's torso in, partially exposing the inner workings of his chest. Looking down at the same hands that tore through the victim, he saw his hands and arms were littered with new bruises.

He dragged Tuomi's body and shoved it into the closet. Hours dragged on as he paced around the room, wondering what to do now. His thoughts muddled and slowed from the alcohol and lack of sleep. The rum bottle he drank from was missing. Panic soared through him; he began to wonder, obsessively, where it could have gone. Nothing was making sense to him, but what was clear was that he'd savagely beaten Tuomi's body with his bare hands in a haze of anger and rage to the point of breaking bones.

In the afternoon, he slipped out of the hotel room, left the body, made his way to Grand Avenue Mall, purchased a massive suitcase with wheels, and returned to the hotel room, sure to book a second night. He hauled the body from the closet, shoving it into the suitcase. He headed down the stairs with the heavy trunk behind him and hailed a taxi. The driver helped Jeffrey lift the case full of Tuomi's body into the trunk. He gave them his grandmother's address.

While Catherine slept soundly in her room, Jeffrey set the suitcase into the fruit cellar and went to bed. He called off work the next two days.

Thanksgiving was around the corner, and Catherine was eager to have her family over to visit. Jeff was left with no other choice than to leave the suitcase undisturbed until the family visit was finished. Anxiety riddled him as he sat around chatting and visiting, knowing about the secret that lingered only a few feet away. And when the weekend was over, he immediately returned to the cellar to begin disposing of the body.

The process was more than unpleasant. The body had stayed in the suitcase for about a week, and decomposition had begun in full force. The process of getting rid of his victim took two hours to complete. Carefully, Jeffrey started by dismembering the corpse with a knife. The head was removed first; then the blade cut through the stomach. He sliced the skin and muscles into smaller pieces, then shoved it all into garbage bags. Tuomi's skeleton was wrapped into an old sheet to prevent bone fragments from flying into the room as he smashed it to pieces with a sledgehammer. He worked in silence, breaking down the bones, trying to make the horror disappear.

He placed the bags outside to be taken away with the rest of the garbage.

But Dahmer made sure to keep Tuomi's head. He stood over the stove with a large pot, boiling the head in a mixture of soilex and bleach. He stared down at the stove while it cooked in chemicals, waiting to wrap and hide it away in the basement closet. Like he had with his previous victim, Jeffrey used the skull to stare at while he masturbated. It stayed with him as a sexual toy for two weeks, but the boiling and chemicals made the bones brittle, and eventually, Jeffrey smashed it into dust and tossed it out.

When their calls went unanswered, Steve Tuomi's family began searching. They contacted the police in December and filed a missing person report. Tuomi's father drove down from northern Michigan and scoured Milawkee in a desperate attempt to locate his lost son. But their questions and fears wouldn't be answered until 1991 when Dahmer was arrested.

Dahmer was never convicted with the death of Steven Tuomi. Police weren't able to establish a positive link, and his bodywas never found.

Steven Tuomi's murder only became a starting point. If any restraint had remained in Dahmer during the fall of 1987, it was stripped away. As he continued stirring vats of chocolate, the darkness in his heart stirred, turning, twisting until it consumed him wholly.

Grandma's Cellar

Within the walls of the Ambrosia Chocolate Factory, Jeffrey Dahmer measured powdered sugar into four massive drums. Mixing the sugar and packs of cocoa powder with heavy machinery, he added the vegetable oil, creating a thick, heavy paste. "A lot of heavy lifting there, a lot of bags to cut open, but it wasn't a bad job," he later described it. When the mixture was ready, he alerted the workers below, and thick globs of brown paste dropped down to be made into chocolate. Jeffrey was a star employee, eager to improve and learn the first several years working, but the other coworkers began to notice his fluctuating stress levels and shift in performance as time went on. He'd fall asleep on the job, dozing off instead of mixing.

His thoughts were muddled, and his mind distracted. For two months, he anxiously waited to see if he'd be connected to Steven Tuomi's death. But not a word was said. Once again, Jeffrey Dahmer successfully committed murder. The feeling of power rushed through him, and that was a stronger feeling than fear.

He'd killed two men without being caught. There was no stopping him now.

It was January 17, 1988, an hour after midnight. On the chilly winter night, fourteen-year-old James Doxtator stood outside the bus station dressed in burgundy jeans, a thick sweater, and a golf cap. He was a bit of a rebel. The police knew Doxtator for car theft, and he'd been arrested a few months prior for hanging around the gay bars late at night. Even though he stood around six feet tall, James was still underage, and he'd often wait around outside clubs to enjoy male company and make some cash.

Jeffrey approached the boy with the offer to pay $50 if James came home with him and posed nude. The fourteen-year-old accepted, and the two rode the bus back to Catherine Dahmer's home in West Allis. She slept soundly while her grandson opened the door and quietly crept into the house with his guest. They stopped in the sitting room and kissed. For over an hour, they undressed and touched one another.

Despite James being underage, Jeff performed oral sex and eventually led James down to the basement. The kissing and touching continued until 4 am, when it all came to a halt. James mentioned he needed to head out. Without revealing his aggravation, Jeff went upstairs to make his signature cocktail—coffee, Irish cream, and sleeping pills. Doxtator drank it without question. All Jeff had to do then was wait for a half-hour to pass until James drifted away beside him into an empty, drug-induced sleep. In the silent home, Jeffrey wrapped his hands around the unconscious fourteen-year-old's neck and strangled him to death.

He didn't want Doxtator to leave.

He dragged the boy's body into the fruit cellar after spreading out a sheet. There Jeff laid down as well, stroking Jame's skin gently and kissing his corpse until the last hours of the night passed, and it was Sunday morning. Catherine woke oblivious to her grandson's devastating night activities. In the crisp morning light, they sat with one another at the table and ate breakfast. She had church that morning, and her grandson would not be joining her. Jeff waited until the car pulled out of the driveway and then returned to the cellar. "I brought him up to the bedroom and pretended he was still alive," he later confessed, adding that he caressed the corpse and sexually assaulted it.

In the cold fruit cellar, Doxtator's body kept for a week. Jeffrey found time to sneak down between long hours at the factory and use the body for whatever fantasy he desired.

Catherine Dahmer began to notice an awful stench permeating her home. She asked Jeff about it, and he told her it was cat litter and that he'd take care of it. It was time to remove the dead body.

In the cellar, he covered the windows, ensuring no unwanted witnesses could peer in. Then he began his process of dismembering Doxtator's body. First, he removed his victim's head, sliced the skin away, and shattered the bones with a sledgehammer to be stuffed into garbage bags and taken by the trash. But the skull was boiled, keeping for two weeks until it became too brittle and fell apart when handled.

The death of James Doxtator was part of an evil hunger in Jeffrey he no longer cared to lock away. The want for a handsome young man to keep and own became an insistent obsession. But not all men joined Jeffrey's sick collection.

It was around this time, Bobby Simpson was out one night when he and Jeffrey Dahmer began talking. The conversation was going well, and after an invitation, they were on a bus back to West Allis. Jeffrey slowly opened the front door, and they tiptoed into the house, careful not to disturb Catherine. They kissed. Jeffrey made drinks, drugging Bobby with sleeping pills, coffee, and Irish cream. After several sips, Bobby blacked out. Jeffrey took in the sight of his new victim. Arousal filled him. He quickly undressed, masturbating four times over Bobby. Eventually, the drugs left Simpson's system, and in a groggy haze, he came to with a naked Jeffrey standing over him. To his shock and horror, it was now 11 am.

He'd been with Jeffrey for hours, but he couldn't remember a single thing. He was allowed to leave that morning.

Later, while out at one of the local bars, Simpson told his story about surviving his night with Dahmer.

"He drugged you too?" a man sitting at the bar asked after overhearing the conversation. During his confession to

Detective Kennedy, Jeff expressed that he had many sexual experiences that didn't end in murder or violence.

But not all of Dahmer's victims shared such luck.

Outside the Phoenix bar two months later, Jeffrey Dahmer met with twenty-three old Richard Guerrero. Dahmer brought up his routine offer of cash for nude photos, which was accepted. They hopped into a cab and stopped at another bar, walking the final two blocks to Jeff's grandmother's home. In Jeff's bedroom, they kissed and pleasured one another. When Guerrero fell asleep, Jeffrey strangled him to death, laying beside his dead body, and for the next several hours, he assaulted it and performed oral on the corpse. In the morning, he ate breakfast with his grandmother while Guerrero's body laid still in his bed. When Catherine left for church, there was no one to disturb Jeff; he returned to the body.

With only a few hours left of alone time, he dismembered the body and set it out to be taken away with the Monday trash collection. Just like his last murder, Jeffrey was able to put up a façade of normalcy for his grandmother.Catherine returned, unaware of what occurred in her home.

Several times a week, Jeffrey Dahmer sat down in front of the television to watch *Return of the Jedi*. He strongly identified with the villain, the Emperor, and went out to purchase a pair of yellow contacts to embody the character. He wore them to the bar, hoping the yellow eyes might bring him some otherworldly power and channel his inner evil sith lord.

But Dahmer needed no help to obtain evil.

It was Easter, and Ronald Flowers's friends invited him for a night out at Club 219. He declined the invitation. The twenty-five-year-old was waiting for a water bed delivery. But when the water bed didn't show, he decided to meet his friends in downtown Milwaukee. He drove himself and planned to drive home. He had to stay sober. When the clubs closed, he and his friends said goodnight and parted ways. Flowers got into his 1978 Oldsmobile Regency, but it failed to start, and after turning the key three times, the battery gave out. There was no other choice but to stand in line at the phone booth and hope someone was still awake to answer. It was hopeless. He was stranded for the night until Jeffrey Dahmer approached him.

"Are you having trouble?" Jeff asked.

Flowers explained to the polite, tall man his predicament.

"I live close by. If you want, we can just go to my house, pick up my car, and come back and then we'll get you going."

"Okay."

He introduced himself as Jeff.

What Ronald didn't know was that Jeff had no car at his grandmother's. They hailed a cab and got inside. Sitting beside Dahmer, Flowers struggled to have a conversation with him. There was a lack of eye contact, and Jeff constantly made negative comments; it was clear he was a depressed person. With only having drunk a single rum and coke, Flowers was sober. He noticed how strange Jeffrey acted upon arriving at his Grandmother's house and that there was no car parked out in the driveway either. Jeff opened the door.

"Is that you, Jeff?" Catherine called down from the stairs.

"Yes, Grandma, I'm just going to make myself a cup of coffee."

Immediately inside, they went into the kitchen, where Jeff brought out a bottle of liquor. Ronald declined quickly.

"I already told you, I'm here to get my car, and that's it."

"Okay, I understand. But I'm going to make myself a cup of coffee."

Jeffrey made a pot and poured two cups. He gave one to Ronald, whose suspicion only grew. He noticed how nervous his host had become. Eager to leave, Flowers sipped the coffee quickly.

"Okay, let's go," Ronald said after finishing the cup.

"Well, just a minute."

Ronald Flowers later described how then Jeff was "staring at me in a way that was scary; it was almost like he was waiting for something to happen." It was the first moment he gave Ronald direct eye contact, waiting for the drugs to take effect.

A wave of dizziness overcame Flowers. He fell forward from his seat, and the last thing he remembered seeing was Jeffrey's shoes then the ground. He passed out, only to wake up in the hospital after being discovered unconscious in a field. He had no drugs in his system or sign of sexual assault, no recollection of what happened or how Jeffrey may have used him. His brother picked him up from the hospital after being discharged.

He didn't know it at the time, but they'd meet again later that summer.

At home, he noticed strange bruises on his neck and that his underwear was on inside out. He filed a complaint to the police, who followed up by speaking with Jeffrey Dahmer. Jeff quickly denied the allegations. Flowers had drunk too much in his version, and he helped take him to the bus station. There was no way to prove either story. The matter was dropped.

But chance would put them together once again.

At Club 219, Ronald Flowers caught sight of Jeffrey Dahmer. All it took was one glance down at Jeff's hush puppies, and Flowers knew it was his attacker. He walked up to him and asked Jeff if he remembered. Jeff told him apathetically he did not and proceeded to invite him back to his place for some coffee. Anger tore through Flowers. "You know who the fuck I am!" he screamed, ready to fight. But his friends got to him and pulled him away. As he headed out that night from the club, he saw Jeffrey hailing a cab with another young man standing beside him. "Don't go with him. He's fucking crazy," Flowers shouted out. The young man stopped, backing away from Jeffrey, oblivious to the nightmare that he narrowly escaped.

The police visit to West Allis after Flowers was enough for the Dahmer family. It was time Jeff moved out of his grandmother's house. The drunken late nights and random visitors put her on edge. She noticed Jeff's strange behavior and items related to the occult; it terrified her.

"There was pressure from my grandma and dad and my aunt Eunice. I guess you could say I was sort of eased out," Jeffrey said.

Cold Blue Eyes

With Richard Guerrero's skull packed up, Jeffrey moved out of his grandmother's house on September 26, 1988, and into a small apartment on 808 North 24th Street. It was a worn-down, brick building, closer to work. He purchased a black table and two griffin statues, with the plan to create a sanctuary for himself and his victims. Without his caring grandmother around, there were no boundaries or rules. In his own space, he could craft whatever playland he wanted.

It didn't take long for fantasy to bleed into the real world. The first day out of the charming West Allis home, Jeffrey's cold blue eyes found a student at the Milwaukee School of the Arts: Somsack Sinthasomphone. It was 3:30 pm when Jeff approached the thirteen-year-old. Somsack was walking home from school, and Jeff offered him $50 if he was willing to pose for his camera. He spoke in a soft, nonthreatening voice. Somack came from a large Laotian family that recently moved from Thailand to Milwaukee. Fifty dollars in exchange for some pictures was quick money, made easy enough. The young teenager asked if he needed to pose naked. Jeff told him it didn't matter. "I thought he was nice and just wanted to try out his new camera," Somsack later said. Jeffrey presented himself as nothing more than a friendly, amateur photographer willing to pay his models.

At his apartment, Jeffrey brought out a polaroid camera and began discussing poses with the boy. He suggested Somsack remove his shirt, but the advice was quickly declined. Jeff said it would make the picture better, so Somsack lifted his shirt over his head, revealing his young, hairless torso. "You have a nice body," Jeff complimented, slowly unhinging from his likable persona. "Lie on the bed with your hands behind your head." Somsack obliged, and after a few more photographs were taken, they went into the kitchen where Jeff made a pot of coffee. They shared a cup, though Jeffrey hardly drank anyway, insisting Somsack drink most of his.

After the coffee break, they made their way back into the living room for more photos. This time, Jeff suggested Somsack unzip his pants to expose his underwear, like a true predator readying his next victim. "Look sexier for the pose," Jeff instructed. But Somsack became uneasy at the photographer's request, and he unzipped it halfway. Jeff reached out, pulled down the zipper, along with his pants and underwear, attempting to assault the thirteen-year-old. Frightened and confused, Somsack immediately stopped Jeff as well as the modeling. He said that it was time for him to leave.

"Do me a favor before you leave," Dahmer instructed. "Come and sit beside me." Somsack sat beside him hesitantly. "I want to hear your stomach." Jeff's head fell forward, pressing his ear to Somsack's stomach. He began licking him from his navel down to his groin while Somack became overwhelmed in horror and panic. He shot up from his seat and snatched his backpack. The sleeping pills began to take effect. Upon arriving home at his front door, Somsack could hardly stand upright. He passed out, and when his father couldn't wake him, they realized something was horribly wrong. At the Good Samaritan Hospital, several tests were run, concluding Somsack had been drugged.

His family called the police.

Jeffrey Dahmer was arrested at the Ambrosia Chocolate Factory for Second Degree Sexual Assault and Enticing a Child for Immoral Purposes. The police arrived at 2:30 am. Handcuffed, Jeff walked out of work, mortified that his coworkers witnessed his embarrassing arrest.

The first six days in jail, Jeffrey was fearful for what investigators might find. He'd murdered four people, and the skull of Richard Guerrero was still stored away in his apartment--the same place where the police were currently sniffing around in. While they never found Guerrero's head, they discovered the polaroid camera, photos of Somsack, sleeping pills, and the bottle of Bailey's Irish Cream. He explained to the detectives he was never aware of the boy's age and denied ever kissing or fondling him, though Somsack claimed to have said his age right away. Jeff told them the drugging was not done on purpose and was a complete accident. He always took his prescription from that cup with his coffee, and if Somsack had been drugged, it was from leftover Halcyon residue.

His bail was set to $10,000, which his father paid.

The news of the arrest surprised and angered Lionel Dahmer. Several days after his release, he visited Jeff.

"I'll never do anything like that again, Dad," Jeff lied, apologizing. The shame was evident on his face, as it had been so many other times before. This event was also how Lionel found out his son was gay. "He asked me if I was gay, and I told him, yes, and he accepted it fairly well. He didn't get upset or anything about it. He just acted surprised and wondered why I'd never told him before, and I said I didn't tell him because I was embarrassed," Jeff later described.

On January 30, 1989, Jeff appeared before a judge, pleading no contest to the charge of Second Degree Sexual Assault. The verdict came back guilty, but the judge wanted to wait to serve the sentencing and review the psychological evaluations.

He underwent evaluations. One evaluation by Dr. Goldfarb stated that Dahmer was "a seriously disturbed young man" and "he must be considered impulsive and dangerous." He determined Jeff had several personality disorders. His depression worsened. The conviction sat like a heavyweight upon Dahmer, pulling him down deeper. Thoughts of suicide began. He moved out of his tiny apartment, returning for a stay with his grandmother, unsure what his sentence would hold.

On March 25, five days into a ten-day vacation, he made his way to Richard's Pharmacy to refill his sleeping pill prescription, and later that night, he went out for drinks with no plans to murder or bring anyone home.

Except when he arrived at the bar, La Cage, the handsome, aspiring model, Anthony Sears, known by friends as Tony, approached the quiet, young man while his friend Jeff Connor stood nearby chatting with an acquaintance.

Sears asked if he had any coke on him. Jeff responded that he had a coke and rum. "No!" Sears said, "I mean cocaine." They continued chatting, and there was no doubt, Jeff was flattered by the sudden attention. Sears was his first victim to approach him—picked from out of the crowd. Jeff invited them back to his grandmothers, telling Sears and Connor he was from Chicago and was up at a visit to see his grandma. Sears accepted, and Connor offered to drive them both. They left the bar area and hopped into Connor's car. It was late when Sears slid into the backseat with Jeff. The whole while, Connor was uneasy. Something seemed off about this guy that he and Sears had picked up, but he didn't want to interfere, even while Sears unzipped Dahmer's pants and began to perform oral.

The car stopped at 57th avenue; Jeff got out of the car first. Connor turned to face his friend and hurriedly expressed his concern. There wasn't much time. Sears promised to call him in a few hours, then Connor could come pick him up.

It was after 3 am when they snuck into Catherine's home and headed downstairs. Together on the bed, they began to kiss and touch, pleasuring one another. Jeffrey started to ask Sears how long he'd stay and if he might be able to come back. The answer was no, and Sears had to get going soon. Connor was waiting up for a call to come pick him up.

It was the wrong answer. Jeffrey went to the kitchen then and made a drink. He waited for the drugs to do their magic; he kissed the sleeping young man then strangled him, proceeding to sexually assault his corpse.

Catherine Dahmer woke up that Sunday morning, once again unaware a dead man laid in her home. She readied herself for church, had breakfast, and was out the door. It gave Jeff a few more hours to be with Sear's body and use it to pleasure himself, though it was not as much time as he would have liked. His grandma would be home soon. He hauled the body upstairs into the bathroom, laying him out in the tub, hoping to have an easier time draining the blood. First, he removed the head and genitals, storing them in a separate bag. Then with a knife, he flayed the skin piece by piece. Everything was smashed, aside from the head and penis, to be thrown out. Jeffrey had grown a special attachment to Anthony Sears, and the following day he called a local hardware store seeking advice on how to dry out a rabbit skin best. Acetone was the secret ingredient.

He went out and purchased a 10-gallon plastic bucket, dumping it full of acetone. For a week, Anthony Sears' head and penis were stored in the tub with the chemical in the bedroom closet. The acetone worked, pulling the fat and water from the flesh to preserve and dry it. He bought makeup to help make everything look alive. Like he had used his previous victims' body parts, Sears' body parts were used for Jeffrey's sexual gratification.

Jeff Connor waited that Sunday morning for a call, but it never came. He drove around West Allis, searching for his friend but had no clue what home belonged to Jeff from Chicago. Karolee Lodahl stopped by Sears's apartment after not hearing from him. She found that his pets, whom he loved dearly, hadn't been fed. She reported him missing. Jeff Connor provided a description and name, but it wasn't enough, and the police pursued the case no further.

Jeffrey was disappointed with the way Sears's head began to shrivel and dry out, looking less and less normal. He stored it in a double-locked case, but with his sentencing hearing around the corner, he feared its discovery. Jeffrey went out and purchased an oval Samsonite cosmetic case, placed the head and genitals into it, and stored it within his work locker at the Ambrosia Chocolate Factory.

The day before his court appearance, Lionel arrived to go with Jeff to court. They stood in his basement bedroom, where Jeff finished packing up his clothes. Lionel caught sight of a square foot, wooden box tightly locked. He asked Jeff what was inside.

"Nothing," Jeff answered.

"Open it up, Jeff."

A flickering moment of controlled agitation and nerves passed Jeff's face. He waited, and his father demanded he revealed the box's contents.

"But why, Dad? There's nothing in it." His agitation grew, and he asked his dad to give him space. Lionel remained firm in his position. In a tantrum, Jeff pulled out a birthday check, recently written by his father, and tore it shreds, claiming if he couldn't get any space, he didn't want the check. A moment of silence passed, then he calmed, explaining it was only pornography, and he didn't want to open it up with his grandmother around. He'd show Lionel in the morning.

The next day, before arriving at his sentencing, Jeff opened the box. Lionel peered in to find a stack of porn magazines. Together they left for court.

Jeffrey was sentenced to one year at the House of Correction but was given work release. He'd work at Ambrosia Chocolate Factory six days a week.

He was allowed ten hours to visit his family for Thanksgiving, but the shame upon returning to West Allis was too much. He wandered the streets, happy to find the bars were still open. He hopped from bar to bar, ending up at Club 219, where he struck up a conversation with a man in his late thirties to early forties. The two began to drink heavily, sipping on strong whiskey. At some point, he lost his memory of the night and blacked out from overdrinking. He recalled waking up in the morning, hogtied in the stranger's apartment. Hooks and ropes kept him bound and suspended from the ceiling, and he was entirely at this stranger's mercy. The man stood beside him, spanking and sexually assaulting Jeff with a white striped candle.

Screams and curses poured from Jeff's mouth, and the man quickly untied him. "I made enough noise, I was yelling loud enough, that he took me down," he said. Jeff gathered his clothing, but the man attempted to stop him.

"What's your hurry? Let's stop and talk about this." He offered to make breakfast.

But Jeff was in no mood for any further conversation and bolted out the door, rushing back to the House of Correction. He was five hours late, and it wasn't until the afternoon the following day that six inches of candle came out of him with his next bowel movement.

His time at the House of Correction ended on March 20, 1990, two months early, and his five-year probation began the moment he stepped out the front door. As far as Jeff was concerned, being on probation meant nothing.

Apartment 213

Anthony Sears's parts were waiting for him patiently, right where he left them in the locker. Now free, he brought them home. He'd found that the penis had stored nicely, but a nasty mold grew over the head. "I took a knife and cut the scalp part off and peeled the flesh off the bone and kept the skull and the scalp." In front of the stove, he boiled a pot of water,, dropping the skull into the raging hot water. Jeffrey described his disturbing ritual: "It actually worked quite well, as you can see from the pictures. When they were dried I could wear his scalp. It would help me to fantasize and remember the night with him. I could suck on his penis and masturbate."

It was time for Jeffrey to find his own apartment. He took a day to look around for a one-bedroom with cheap rent and close to the bus line as well as work. He settled on the Oxford Apartments on North 25th Street. No. 213. With a monthly rent of $300 and completely furnished, Jeff decided it was worth the risk of the neighborhood. Positioned right in one of the most dangerous parts of Milwaukee, drug-related crime was a daily occurrence. It was a place few cops choose to visit if they had a choice. For Jeffrey, it was affordable, liveable, and it gave him the privacy he craved. On May 14, he moved in with what little belongings he had, making sure to bring Sears's scalp, skull, and penis.

He joined the Unicorn Bath Club in Chicago, taking a total of ten trips down for visits. No one claimed to have been drugged by him and no police reports were filed involving Jeffrey.

He painted Sear's skull gray in his leisure time, readying it for display on his grand shrine. That goal had not been forgotten.

And though his apartment neighbors thought Jeff was fine and pleasant enough, they were clueless to the acts behind his door, only walls apart from them.

During the summer, Jeffrey Dahmer met Ramond Smith, a thirty-two-year-old nicknamed Ricky Beeks, outside near Club 219. Smith was asex worker, and though he didn't consider himself gay, he was willing to sleep with men in exchange for payment. He was good-looking and had a muscular build, matching Jeff's preferred type. Jeff approached him with the line of taking pictures and paying him $50. He mentioned they might watch some porn and have a drink.

Smith agreed, and they left for the new apartment, stopping the taxi to pick up some cigarettes on their way.

Like so many of his victims, Jeffrey didn't want them to leave him. But Smith made it clear that it would cost a lot more than $50 to keep him around. Jeff promised to pay. He'd just have to wait until morning and then made his way to the kitchen. He crafted his sleeping potion, ensuring there were enough pills to do the job. He handed the potion to Smith, and then the waiting game began. It didn't take long. Smith passed out in thirty minutes. Jeffrey wrapped his hands tightly around Smith's throat, strangling him to death.

Now, in the privacy of his own apartment, he could play and experiment. He laid out Smith's body on the large black table, rearranging it into a perfect pose to photograph with his polaroid camera.

But the clean-up and dismemberment were far more of a chore in his second-story apartment than at his grandmother's. He moved the corpse to the bathroom and began dissection. First, he cut off the legs from the pelvis, using an eighty-gallon steel kettle of water and Soilex to boil the legs down. Soilex is a harsh chemical commonly used to remove wallpaper before painting. After an hour, he rinsed the legs then stripped away any extra flesh.

The next day Jeff purchased a large freezer intending to keep the body, but it quickly fell apart. He used a massive trash container with a tight lid filled with strong acid to dispose of it. "I waited a week or two, and they had all turned to slush at that time, which I scooped out with a smaller trash thing and poured it into the toilet and flushed it down. It was just all slush, black slush," Jeff later described.

He placed the freshly painted skull beside Anthony Sears's, the newest addition to his trophies. The paint made them look like nothing more than harmless Halloween decorations.

A week passed. Jeffrey opened his apartment door, inviting in his newest guest. While they chatted, he pulled out the coffee maker and brewed a fresh pot, slipping his recently filled prescription of sleeping pills into the cup. But at some point during the exchange, whether it was intended or not by the guest, the cups of coffee were switched. Jeff experienced what so many of his victims went through. His head became heavy and sluggish as he blacked out. He'd ingested the full dose of drugs. When he woke, he discovered the man had run off, taking $300, clothes, and a watch.

Jeff told the story to his probation officer, Donna Chester. The encounter had left him visibly upset, and she noticed how unkempt he appeared. While Jeff slacked on meetings with his probation officer, he'd also let his personal hygiene go out the window, caring little to shower or clean his clothes, and failed to attend his mandatory group therapies. Chester had been excused from making home visits with Dahmer due to her massive caseload and the fact he lived in a dangerous neighborhood. But when they did meet, it was clear that he was sinking into a depressive state that only pushed him deeper to darkness.

In May, Ted Frankforth caught his friend, twenty-eight-year-old Eddie Smith, locked in conversation with a blonde stranger out at a bar. He approached them, introducing himself. In the fray of the club, drinks, and loud music, Franforth lost sight of Dahmer and Smith.

Eddie Smith was a social man with high ambitions to one day become famous. An ex-dancer, he had once tried to land a spot in the Milwaukee ballet. During the summer of 1990, Eddie mentioned on several occasions a movie producer he'd met who would help move his career forward. A witness later saw the two of them in Juneau Park together. The following two months, he spoke about the movie producer to friends and family, mentioning to the bartender he thought Jeff was cute.

It was on June 24 when Eddie made the fatal trip to Jeff's apartment to take pictures. They had oral sex, then Jeff provided a drug-filled concoction and strangled Eddie to death. He'd fallen into a consistent pattern with his victims. After luring them to his apartment, he'd drug them then strangle them. Only after murdering his victims could he experiment.

Jeff considered Eddie's murder to be a waste and felt "rotten" about the whole encounter. Not because he felt guilty, though--to Jeffrey, it was a waste because he was unable to save any of the body parts as several of his experiments went wrong. Most noticeably was the attempt of drying the skull out in the oven; instead of drying out, it ended up exploding into pieces. He was left with no choice but to drown the remains in a chemical brew and flush the liquified contents down the toilet.

From a close family with nine children, Eddie's death did not go unnoticed. Months after his disappearance, his brother stood at the corner of the bars, holding photos of Eddie, asking desperately if any had seen his lost brother.

They would not get an answer for another year.

In April, Eddie Smith's sister, Carolyn, answered the phone. It was "a male caucasian," someone she'd never met, who told her, "Don't bother looking for your brother; he's dead."

Fifteen-year-old Luis Pinet swept the floors of Club 219, clearing tables and wiping glasses. He worked part-time as a busboy and into the late nights. Dahmer noticed him several times before, assuming he was of age, and on July 6, 1990, they finally spoke to one another at the Phoenix Tavern after Club 219 was closed.

He propositioned the teenager with $200 to come back to his place and pose nude for photos. For Jeff, $200 was what it would take him to pose nude, so he bumped up the offer. Pinet agreed, and the two got into a taxi and made their way to the Oxford apartments.

Jeff pulled out his polaroid camera, snapping several shots, then "light sex" followed. The hours passed, and unlike the others, Pinet stayed the whole night sleeping soundly beside the killer. In the morning, Pinet agreed to come back, and a time was set. He'd meet Jeff at twelve o'clock the following day then left without being paid.

Jeff was thrilled by a second date. He wanted to keep the teenager for himself like his other possessions. Upon their next meeting, a plan was created; he'd murder him, though he was out of sleeping pills and at the time couldn't afford a refill. Jeff decided to beat Pinet over the head with a hammer after getting him blackout drunk. That morning, he purchased a rubber mallet.

Twelve o'clock in the afternoon rolled around, and Jeffrey arrived at their agreed meeting place, ready to enact his next fantasy. But Jeffrey described his disappointment: "He didn't show up, so I thought he was just kidding; he's not going to meet me."

Later that night, they ran into one another outside the Phoenix Tavern. Pinet explained he completely misunderstood Jeff. He thought they were meeting at midnight, not during the day, and he never planned to back out on the encounter. Relief flooded Jeffrey: he hadn't been abandoned, and now he would have his chance with Pinet. After speaking, they returned to the Oxford apartments where drinks were had. Eventually, Jeff brought out his camera and instructed Pinet to strike a particular pose on the mattress while shooting. The fifteen-year-old laid face down on the mattress drunk, utterly unaware that Jeffrey stood behind him, a rubber mallet in hand. With a swift, hard blow, he slammed the hammer against the back of Pinet's neck.

"Pat, do you know what happens when you hit someone on the head with a rubber mallet? Well, they get mad at you," Jeffrey Dahmer told Detective Patrick Kennedy.

After being struck, Luis Pinet jerked up off the bed and demanded an explanation. Jeffrey quickly explained he only feared Pinet would leave with the $200 without a fair exchange. The fifteen-year-old accepted Jeff's excuse, didn't push the matter any further, and hurried out the door. Ten minutes passed. Jeff opened the front door after hearing a knock to find Pinet. He needed some cash to get a bus ride home.

It was another golden opportunity; Jeff still intended to kill Pinet. Out of fear of losing him one more time, Jeffrey attacked him again. The two locked into a physical altercation on the floor, wrestling one another. Dahmer managed to wrap his hands around his throat, but Luis was too strong, and Dahmer gave up.

"Let's talk," he said, pulling away from the fight. They calmed down, sitting on the edge of the bed. Through their discussion, Dahmer managed to bind Pinet's hands behind his back, but the teenager was quick and aware at this point. He slipped out of the bonds and attempted to leave. In a fit of desperation, Jeff grabbed the knife used so often to slice through flesh and forced Pinet to promise he'd never tell a soul about tonight. Pinet swore he wouldn't. The busboy left, luck on his side, and they never spoke to one another again.

The next day, Dahmer arrived at his meeting with his probation officer an hour late. Chester noticed he "looked rough." He told her he'd overslept, fell down the stairs, and hurt himself.

On a late summer night in early September, Jeff walked out of the bars and headed to an adult bookstore on one of Milwaukee's main streets around 3 am. He ran into the handsome and well-built Ernest Miller. Immediately, Jeff's interest was piqued. Ernest Miller was, in fact, one of the best-looking men he'd ever seen. He gave his usual offer of $50, and the two walked a few blocks back to Apartment 213.

It was all a well-rehearsed routine.

Miller laid down, and Jeffrey listened intently to his stomach and chest, lavishing in the man's internal sounds and beating heart. He pressed his lips to Miller's skin then slowly kissed his way down to Miller's groin, but was interrupted. It would cost more than $50 if Jeff wanted to move any further. He got up then and went to the kitchen, mixing rum, coke, and two sleeping pills. Miller took the drink and drifted into a dark empty sleep. Jeff was pleased with himself, staring at the handsome unconscious man. Miller was what he considered almost ideal. His fingers brushed along Miller's warm flesh, and he masturbated over him. Several times he walked around his apartment sipping on cold beers. He took hours, keeping him alive a bit longer than the others to savor every second.

He knew two pills were not enough. His time was limited, and strangling Miller might wake him up, and then there'd be a fight. Based on Miller's build, Jeff knew he wouldn't stand a chance. He reached for his dissecting knife, the same one he forced Luis Pinet with, and carefully slit Miller's jugular. Red blood seeped into the room and floor, leaving permanent stains for the police to one day find. It was a quick and almost instant death.

He moved the body and set it up in the apartment. His camera at the ready, snapping photo after photo, he repositioned Miller's body to his morbid delight. Finished with capturing memories, he brought the body into the bathroom.

There, his usual process of dismemberment began. Once he removed the head, he pressed it to his lips, whispering and apologizing. He snapped more photographs and placed the head in the refrigerator.Jeffrey later explained in detail how he mutilated the body: "I separated the joints, the arm joints, the leg joints, and had to do two boilings. I think I used four boxes of Soilex for each one, put in the upper portion of the body, and boiled that for about two hours and then the lower portion for another two hours. The Soilex removes all the flesh, turns it into a jelly-like substance, and it just rinses off. Then I laid the clean bones in a diluted bleach solution, left them there for a day and spread them out on either newspaper or cloth, and let them dry for about a week in the bedroom." Other parts of the body, like the liver, arms, and kidney, were preserved in the freezer. The skeleton he saved to put back together and relive the moment. It aroused him greatly, and he was able to use pieces of Miller to satisfy him.

But during this time, Jeffrey needed more of a rush. Killing and photos were no longer enough. He needed more. More ways to keep his victims with him--in him.

"That's when the cannibalism started," he later said.

The heart came first. He described the texture as spongey. Then he tasted the thigh, realizing the muscle was too tough to chew, so before he had any of the biceps, which he thought were stunning, a meat tenderizer was purchased.

Two weeks after being reported missing, Ernest Miller's grandmother claimed to have received an anonymous phone call. The voice on the other line let out a series of moans and, in a faint whisper, repeated "help."

Upon questioning, Jeffrey Dahmer denied ever calling his victim's families.

Murderous Routine

David Thomas was another victim who disappeared to Dahmer's routine. He was twenty-two years old when he was last seen September 24, 1990, and currently on probation for shoplifting. At the time, he floated around, staying with his girlfriend for short periods of time as they had a rocky relationship. He visited his three-year-old daughter often.

He met Jeffrey out during the day and was coerced into returning back to the apartment with him, where he was drugged and eventually fell asleep. During it all, Jeff realized "he wasn't my type." But he couldn't let him wake up and risk being reported. In Jeff's twisted mind, murder was the only solution.

He dismembered the body, well-practiced at the task now, ensuring to snap a variety of photos from start to finish. He told detectives by the seventh murder that he was rather efficient. All of Thomas's remains were turned to slush and poured down the toilet. His body was never recovered.

That Thanksgiving Shari and Lionel made the trip to visit Jeff and Catherine. They were celebrating in West Allis that afternoon. Jeff arrived late. He was well dressed, and his hair neatly combed. He spoke to his family about having acquired an interest in aquariums and fish; at one point, he laid on the floor to play with his grandmother's orange tabby. He answered questions about his apartment, work, and what he did in his free time, all without missing a beat.

And when Shari and Lionel stopped by that day to check out his new apartment, Jeff provided a tour with confidence. It was tidy and neat, and there wasn't much furniture. Jeff had a beige couch pushed up against the wall as well as a chair in the living room. The only thing that didn't make sense to Lionel and Shari was the freezer. They asked why he bought it. Jeff casually explained it was to stock up on sale items. It was a sensible reason. And when asked about the lock on the bedroom and bathroom door, Jeff told them it was extra security since robberies were common in the neighborhood.

What Jeffrey didn't explain then was how his life was becoming a haze of monotony. Every day was a carbon copy of working long hours and drinking away his free time. In his mind, he had little to offer for his family. He told his parole officer, his father is "controlling, and he has nothing in common with the brother who attends college, and he is embarrassed about his offense."

Taking care of his fish became a hobby he loved. From the Fish Factory, Jeff purchased a thirty-gallon tank. It sat upon the future altar table with tropical fish swimming around in it. For Jeffrey, it was his one ordinary hobby, something he truly had fun with, and after his arrest, a hobby he missed. "It was nice, with African cichlids and tiger barbs in it and live plants; it was a beautifully kept fish tank, very clean . . . I used to like to just sit there and watch them swim around, basically. I used to enjoy the planning of the set-up, the filtration, read about how to keep the nitrate and ammonia down to safe levels and just the whole spectrum of fish-keeping interested me."

But the fish tank wasn't enough to occupy all his free time or his heinous needs. "I should have gone to college and gone into real estate and got myself an aquarium, that's what I should have done," he later reflected.

Seventeen-year-old Curtis Straughter met Dahmer at a bus station in February of 1991. He was a high school dropout with plans to become a model, but in the meantime, he worked as a nursing assistant and loved to write music. It was a cold winter evening when Jeff made his way to the station to get downtown; there Straughter sat. Jeff started up a conversation while they waited, and the offer to head to the apartment and watch a movie was made. Jeff hinted at the possibility of sex.

It wasn't long until the two walked back to Jeff's. He threw a movie on and made a drink laced with pills. Soon Straughter was out cold, and Jeff kissed and cuddled his body after sexually assaulting him. Because his prescription had run low, Dahmer feared his victim would wake up early. He took a leather strap and strangled the teenager to death.

Straughter's head, hands, and genitals were saved and added to the collection. He wanted to preserve the genitals for future oral sex and soaked them in formaldehyde for two weeks.

During this time, Jeffrey discovered he most enjoyed human flesh sauteed with mushroom and onion. To him, it tasted like an expensive filet mignon.

Errol Lindsey was only nineteen when he was strangled on April 7. He was the youngest of six children and last seen by his mother when he left to get a key made. It was near the key shop where Jeffrey made his typical advance. They were only two blocks from his apartment, and after luring Lindsey there, Jeff laced his drink then murdered him. He assaulted Lindsey, performing oral upon the body. For two hours, Dahmer took the time to skin the corpse. He described the process similar to how one might flay a chicken; the hardest part was around the eyes and mouth. After removing the skin around the face, he wrapped it around his own like a mask. It was an attempt to connect with his victim, to become one. He desired to preserve the skin, soaking it in a solution of salt and water, but he quickly learned the skin disintegrated and could not be an addition to his shrine. He kept the flayed body, laying it out on a sheet and photographing it after severing the hands.

Jeffrey always had a supply of Bud Light to drink as he went through his process of dismemberment. The smell was awful. On several different occasions, the apartment manager approached Jeff and asked about the stench; several of the other tenants made complaints. Jeff explained his fish tank's motor had broken while he was on a visit to Chicago, and several fish died. The manager told him to throw it all out. "From then on, I was always trying to eliminate the odors with fans, cleansers, and air fresheners."

But as much as it was a sexual experience, dismemberment was chore-like. He relied on the alcohol to get him through it before the remorse set in of losing another possession.

Naked, he stood over his victim's body to refrain from staining his clothes with any blood. With their bodies positioned face up above the drain, he made a long incision from the sternum down and opened up the torso, removing the internal organs. At times, the sight of the insides aroused him to the point he stopped and reached orgasm by "stimulating intercourse with the viscera."

"I noticed that all the blood tends to collect in the chest area, so I drained that off. You just lift the torso part, and it drains out down the bathtub drain. Then you slice up the liver into smaller pieces; it's quite large. You start cutting off the flesh in the leg area or the arm area and just work your way down. Then when I was saving the heads, I'd cut the neck bone, sever the head," Jeffrey later explained.

After taking what pieces of flesh and body he wanted to save, the rest of the remains were dumped into the barrel and soaked in acid.

On May 4, 1991, a hard, heavy knock banged on his door. It was the police. Twenty-six-year-old Dean Vaughn, who lived above Jeff, had been found dead in his apartment. He'd been strangled to death and was last seen by two neighbors with another subject around 12:30 am. The police were asking around, and Jeff told them he never heard or saw anything. Vaughn's murder was never solved, but many people his death could be linked to Dahmer.

During that spring, Jeffrey reached a point in his life where the week only existed for him to reach the weekend. He purchased a copy of the 1977 film *The Exorcist II*. Watching it became a daily ritual. He put the VHS in when he returned from work before going to the bars and watched it with his victims. He believed he no longer had a moral compass and had sunk entirely into darkness, welcoming it wholly.

"Usually, I knew when I went out if I was looking to keep someone. Before leaving the apartment, I would crush up five to seven Halcyon tablets in a glass and leave it on the kitchen sink." He'd wait then, scoping out potential victims, plucking out the ones from the crowds who he found attractive and who appeared to be alone.

May 24, Jeff presented a note to thirty-one-year-old Anthony Hughes at Club 219, inviting him back to his apartment. He was immediately attracted to him and made his approach. Jeff was surprised to learn Anthony was deaf and mute. He had contracted pneumonia as a baby, leaving him disabled, but that didn't stop Hughes from living life; he enjoyed the clubs and the loud music reverberation. "I think he could read lips though and we communicated by writing little notes to one another in a small notebook that he had," Jeffrey later recalled. When the club closed, Dahmer wrote down an invitation back to his place for nude photos in exchange for $50. Hughes agreed.

Anthony Hughes' friends were a little hesitant to let their friend leave with Jeff, but he and Jeff both insisted everything would be fine, and so they left that night after close and arrived at 213.

They kissed and touched one another until the sleeping pills worked. Dahmer waited patiently; then, when it was time, he drilled two holes into Hughes' head and with a turkey baster injected a diluted mix of acid. The solution was too strong, and it immediately killed Hughes. Distraught and disappointed, Dahmer drank until he passed out beside the body.

When Dahmer woke, he had too much to do that day and left the body on his bedroom floor. The building manager approached him asking to remove the horrid smell. It was not uncommon for Jeffrey to live among the dead, unbothered by the scent of decomposition and death. Several polaroids include images of the bowels removed from the corpses. Complaint after a complaint came in about the smell, and Jeff was able to provide an excuse, whether it be the fish tank or his freezer. He was unphased by what made others nauseous, sleeping within his apartment death museum. Though there were threats and requests for the smell to leave, nothing was done to reprimand Jeff.

He had no reason to stop.

May 25, 1991, Konerak Sinthasomphone hopped out of the shower and said goodbye to his family and older brother Somsack before heading to a party. It would be the last time they'd see the happy, energetic young teenager.

When asked if Jeff knew the Sinthasomphones were brothers, he was surprised. "Why no, how could I have known? I never inquired into the personal lives of my victims. I really didn't want to know," he later told Detective Kennedy and Murphy.

In that same afternoon, Jeffrey Dahmer said goodbye to the lifeless body of Anthony Hughes, which still remained in the apartment, and went to Grand Avenue Mall. He wandered about for the next five hours with no clear plans. With Hughes' corpse still intact, he had no intention of bringing anyone else home for him to keep. Jeff was sober and not in the mindset to kill, but all of that changed when he caught a glimpse of the fourteen-year-old in shorts and black tennis shoes. He initiated the conversation and proposed the same offer he had with his older brother: money for nude photos. After a bit of reluctance, Konerak agreed.

Jeff plied his victim with pills in the one-bedroom apartment, and while the victim slept, he assaulted him by performing oral. Afterward, Jeff cuddled up beside the boy and slept a few hours. Then he drilled two holes into the boy's head, injecting Muriatic acid, and was pleased to find this time his living zombie experiment didn't immediately die. He left late in the night, around one in the morning, to grab a beer at a local bar.

In his absence, Konerak came to, waking up. He scrambled out of the apartment to be seen by a young couple. He sprinted across the street and ran straight into a tree, clearly disoriented. At first glance, he was merely written off as a drunk. A man helped him up from the ground, and then Tina Spivey, Nicole Childress, and Sandra Smith made their approach to offer aid. He was clearly confused and disoriented; he was unable to speak, sitting on the curbside only to stand and stagger about. He clutched his head in his hands, in tremendous pain. Blood was on his penis and anus, running down his leg. His long dark hair hid some of the damage, and the holes in his head were narrow enough that bleeding out was greatly subdued.

Jeff had not been gone more than half an hour when he decided it would be best to check on his experiment. He left after one drink to turn the corner on his way home and see three women standing around a naked Konerak. Immediately, he had to get the boy away and inside. Upon approaching, he attempted to assure the women he'd take care of the situation, but Konerak refused Jeff, swinging his arms and screaming. At one point, the frightened boy clung to a tree in desperation. The women became seriously alarmed, and when Jeff used three different fake names to try and gain control, it was obvious he was lying.

Without hesitation, Sandra Smith returned home and phoned the police: "Okay. Hi...I'm on 25th and State and there's this young man. He is butt naked. He has been beaten up. He is very bruised up. He can't stand...he has, he is naked, he has no clothes on. And he is really hurt. And I, you know, I ain't got no quarter on him, I just seen him. He needs some help."

At 2:06 am, Officers Joseph Gabrish and John Balcerzak were sent to investigate.

Dahmer's immediate demeanor shifted into calm, quiet, and cooperative. While the three women were certain Konerak was a mere child, Jeffrey assured them he was an adult about nineteen years old and was Jeff's lover, providing a fake name. The lies poured out without hesitation. Jeff explained his lover had too much to drink and ran off. Jeffrey presented his own I.D. and address. He explained Konerak didn't have any identification with him since he only stays with Jeff but doesn't live with him. Konerak leaned against the car door, drugged and suffering brain damage; he could not communicate and defend himself from the monster.

Jeffrey laughed, chuckling with the officers as he explained this was a routine problem of his boyfriend's, mainly when they argued, and when he drank too much, it wasn't uncommon for him to take off all his clothes and run out.

The police decided to trust the helpful and kind man. He was providing answers to the questions in an agreeable manner.

The women were understandably upset. They started to shout in protest at the officers, who both refused to investigate or stop the situation. At one point, the officer told Miss Spivey to "shut the hell up." It was clear the police had little interest in pursuing a case involving gay men and asked Jeff to take Konerak back to the apartment. Konerak struggled, and the cops encouraged Dahmer to be more demonstrative with his partner. They went as far as to grab the fourteen-year-old and help wrangle him half a block back to Dahmer's. Jeff proudly showed the polaroids he snapped of Konerak hours earlier. There he was smiling and in black briefs, verifying the story that they were indeed lovers. There was no sign of struggle. His clothes were even folded neatly on the couch. Konerak sat quietly on the couch in a daze of drugs and acid marinating in his head. In fact, the only off-putting sign was the horrid scent, but that didn't matter. The apartment was old. Of course, had they pressed to see inside the closed door to the bedroom, they would have found the body of Anthony Hughes.

Jeff apologized for the embarrassing, drunken display and continued assuring them there was nothing to be worried about. He wouldn't let it happen again.

"Well, you just take care of him," one said before they both stepped out, leaving with nothing more than a warning. Unbelievably, Jeffrey once again narrowly escaped being caught. The police had been inside his apartment, surrounded by evidence.

Alone, Jeffrey injected another round of acid, hoping to pacify Konerak into a better-suited zombie. But it was too much, and the boy died immediately. Disappointment flooded Jeff, but he wasted no time getting to the dismemberment. He flayed the skin of both Anthony Hughes and Konerak Sinthasomphone simultaneously, bagging it all to be thrown away. He was sure to capture the moment on camera as he went through the process to relive it all. Several of the photos include Konerak's head in the sink, face up, staring at the camera. Others show the viscera exposed and the body cut open from sternum to genitals.

After it all, he made sure to keep the skulls; if he didn't save something, in his mind, it would have been a waste.

At 2:22 am, Officers Joseph Gabrish and John Balcerzak radioed in and said to the dispatcher, "The intoxicated Asian naked male was returned to the sober boyfriend, and we're ten-eight." Laughter came over the radio. Minutes passed, and the dispatcher gave them the next assignment, but they radioed back, "Ten-four. It'll be a minute, my partner's gonna get deloused at the station."

Ms. Cleveland called the police again to find out what happened. She asked if the child was safe and taken care of.

"It wasn't a child. It was an adult," the dispatcher corrected.

"Are you sure?"

"Yup."

Several days passed, and it became increasingly clear Jeff was losing grip on the real world. The fantasy had latched itself fully and ran the show. He was missing too much work and was on the brink of losing his job. His building manager approached him with the warning eviction was on the horizon due to the horrible smell.

He escaped his problems in Milwaukee by taking frequent trips down to Chicago.

Jeffrey Dahmer stood in the rallying crowds of Chicago on June 30, 1991, at a gay pride event. Later in the evening, he headed to an area referred to as "Boys Town" and hit up a few of the popular gay bars. There he met Matt Turner, a handsome man with aspirations to one day be a model, who eagerly accepted having his photo taken. They took the greyhound bus back to Milwaukee and headed to Jeff's apartment. He used the leather strap to strangle Turner, then dismembered him. Turner's head was placed inside a plastic bag stored in the freezer.

Again, he returned to Chicago a week after Turner; this time, he ran into the handsome and charming Jeramiah Weinberger, who was twenty-three at the time. He and Dahmer hit it off at Carol's Speak Easy, a popular gay bar. "He was very affectionate in the bar. He was giving me blow jobs right in the bar and everything," Jeffrey claimed. They retreated to a backlit area to fool around, afterward returning to the main area to sit with others. Weinberger plopped himself on top of Dahmer's lap, excitedly talking and flirting. Jeff loved the outward affection, something he rarely received, and like so many times before, he presented an invitation back to his place. Weinberger asked his close friend, Ted Jones, "This guy wants me to leave here and go to Milwaukee for the weekend. What do you think?" Ted looked Jeff up and down. "He looks okay, go for it. You don't have anything else to do this weekend."

It was close to four in the morning when Ted Jones said his final goodbye. "I'll call you tomorrow to see if you want to go to a picnic this weekend. If there's no answer, I'll assume you went for the weekend." They parted ways, and Jeff brought his next victim home.

They spent the weekend together, and to Jeff, it was as if a real relationship was starting. They made love, went out to the mall, and cooked together. Jeffrey mulled over the idea perhaps they might turn into something real, more than anything he'd had yet. But Sunday night came, and at the mention of leaving for work in the morning back in Chicago, the fear of abandonment returned, and the flip switched.

Losing Weinberger was something Jeff couldn't fathom, but he wanted to keep him alive as long as possible.

After he was drugged, Jeff began his experimentation. He drilled two holes into Weinberger's head, but this time he didn't use any acid, he stuck to boiling hot water. It worked. A poorly done lobotomy such as this can cause mental dullness, loss of personality, and loss of independence. Dahmer successfully recreated the childlike, mute, and docile nature of the lobotomies performed in the 1940s.

"He woke up at the end of the day, the next morning, and he was sort of groggy and everything. He talked, it was like he was dazed and I thought I would be able to keep him that way," Jeffrey explained. Weinberger was alive and in a zombie state for Jeffrey to use however he pleased. Weinberger shuffled about the apartment in a foggy, indecisive state, unsure what had happened. Jeff helped him shower; there was no sign Weinberger was going to escape.

But Jeff had work and didn't want to risk Weinberger running out like Konerak. He gave him another round of sleeping pills, injecting more boiling water into his brain, then left for work. After his shift, he was disappointed to find Weinberger dead on the floor, his eyes wide open, staring blankly back at him.

Jeff began his process of taking photos. He severed the head, leaving it a mixture of bleach and water for a whole week. Weinberger's was a death Jeff would later openly regret.

His mental state continued to take a sharp decline. His work and process had become lazy and sloppy. He told Donna Chester on July 8 that he was close to being fired and once he lost his job, then he'd have a good reason to commit suicide.

Completely out of control, he continued.

After recently moving to Milwaukee with his fiance, Rose Colon, the handsome and athletic Oliver Lacy had a run-in with Jeffrey Dahmer. He had a two-year-old son and plans to move forward in life.

Jeffrey ran into him on July 15, 1991, right around the corner from the Oxford apartments. Lacy was on his way to visit his cousin but was lured back to the apartment after showing Jeff some pictures of him modeling. Dahmer was beside himself: "He was extremely handsome."

According to Jeff, the two took off their clothes and began to rub their bodies against one another. After consuming a drugged drink, Lacy passed out, and Dahmer killed him and assaulted his corpse. Jeff described taking his time with Lacy, as the mere sight of him excited him greatly. The head was stored in a box within the fridge, and the heart was kept in the freezer "to eat later." Jeff wanted to keep as much of him as he could, going as far as to keep his I.D.

Lacy's family became extremely worried when Oliver never returned from work that day.

Collapsing Fantasy

"As I told you yesterday, the company has completed its investigation and has decided to convert your suspension to a termination for excessive absenteeism. Jeff, it is truly unfortunate that you did not take corrective action to improve your attendance record. This is something that you alone control. If you have any personal belongings on company property please arrange for its removal no later than July 25, 1991." Jeff stared at the letter received from Ambrosia Chocolate Factory on July 19, 1991.

His time there was over. He would lose his apartment soon.

His mental state was progressively dissolving into one run by compulsion and desire.

The day earlier, he'd been rejected by Ricky Thomas for a few drinks back at his apartment. His probation officer noticed how tense and uneasy Jeff appeared in the next meeting. He told her he'd been drinking beer nonstop since losing his job. It had been three days since killing Lacy, and he hadn't showered or bathed once. His clothes were dirty and his face unshaven. He yawned constantly. She provided several suggestions and offered information about The Salvation Army in case he became homeless.

But Jeff was far beyond help.

On July 19, while riding the bus, Jeff's icy blue eyes caught twenty-five-year-old Joseph Bradehoft waiting at a bus stop with a six-pack of beer tucked beneath his arm. Jeff got off the bus and struck up the offer to come back to his place. Bradehoft, who was in town visiting his brother, agreed.

There at 213, he was drugged then murdered. His head was stored in the freezer along with Weinberger's.

Within the confines of the one-bedroom, Jeffrey kept both Oliver Lacy and Bradehoft's bodies. He posed them for photographs, at one point hanging Lacy's headless body by a strap from the shower rod. He had previously positioned Lacy's body on top of Weinberger. A playland of his fantasy, he lived among the death and destruction caused by his hands. Eviction was on the horizon, and he cared little to clean up his mess. There was no point. He showered with Oliver Lacy and

Bradehoft's corpses, standing over them as the water ran down. Heads were placed in the freezer. Hearts and biceps were fried up and eaten. A bag of organs was stuck to the bottom of the freezer, waiting for consumption. The blue drum in the corner of his room held a concoction of chemicals and three people. Bradehoft was left on the bed for several days with a sheet pulled over the body. Their Jeffrey could lay beside him at night and sleep, cozied up until he discovered maggots inside the head. He severed and cleaned it, then placed it within the freezer beside the others.

"Nothing else gave me pleasure towards the end, nothing, not the normal things, especially near the end when things just started piling up, person after person, during the last six months. I could not get pleasure from going out to eat. I just felt very empty, frustrated, and driven to continue doing it...I was just driven to do it more frequently and more frequently until it was just too much – complete overload. I couldn't control it anymore," Jeffrey later said.

He had killed and mutilated four men in three weeks.

July 22, 1991, was a lazy, warm afternoon. Jeffrey wandered near the bus station, approaching men with the offer to come back to his place and watch a few movies. He was declined twice and made his way to the Grand Avenue Mall. He approached a sixteen-year-old, then another man in the bathroom, both of whom rejected his invitation to watch movies at his place. It was only 3:30 in the afternoon.

After eating a pizza and a quick beer, he caught sight of three men gathered together. One was Tracy Edwards, who recently moved to Milwaukee. He'd met Tracy Edwards in passing; once he bummed a cigarette off him. He struck up a conversation along with Edward's two friends, expressing that he was bored and was willing to pay them each $100 to come back to his place and watch movies. They asked if he wanted sex too; the only stipulation Jeffrey had is he wanted to handcuff one of them. The three men agreed. It was quick money. Though at this point, Jeff was flat out broke and had been warned of imminent eviction from his apartment.

Though, according to Edwards, when Jeff approached he invited them all to a party back at his place and even mentioned his girlfriend would be there.

They walked a few blocks and stopped at a liquor store on 7th street. Jeff bought a six-pack of beer. It was around 6 pm when the group started to dissipate. The two friends headed off in search of finding some girls to talk to. Jeff and Tracy hopped into a cab. The group was now separated, and the friend had no idea where Edwards was heading. Jeff had lied and told them he lived at the Ambassador Hotel.

And while Tracy and Dahmer arrived at Oxford apartments, the two friends made their way to the Ambassador Hotel, only to wait cluelessly on where the bored stranger had taken Tracy. Their fears and worries only grew as time passed.

Before entering the apartment, Tracy stood watching as Jeff messed with a security system before they entered. Red flags began to pop up. Although the place was neat and orderly, there was no denying the foul smell lingering in the air. It was hot inside, and the stench baked into the walls and heat. Edwards asked about the bottles of Muriatic acid resting on the floor; Jeff told him it was for cleaning bricks.

While answering questions, he had to think of a plan. Jeff was out of Halcyon.

Tracy bent down and examined the fish swimming inside the tank when suddenly he felt a handcuff slapped on his wrist. He turned around.

"What's happening?" Tracy asked. Jeff tried to play it off as a joke and said they could get the key from the bedroom. He opened the door. The Exorcist II played in the background on the VCR as if it were waiting for them. He saw the massive blue barrel sitting in the corner, beneath posters of naked men. Jeff told him he wouldn't get hurt if he just posed nude with the handcuffs on. Between the stifling heat, horrible scent, and the strange behavior of his host, Edwards had to get out.

He knew he was in danger. Dahmer insisted handcuffs were necessary for him to be in control. At one point, Jeff pulled a skull from a filing cabinet and began to rub himself with it, all while telling Edwards how he too would be staying.

When Tracy refused to be handcuffed or remove his clothes, Dahmer pulled out a knife. On high alert, Tracy attempted to relax Jeff, agreeing to remove his clothes and pose if Jeff put the knife away. Satiated, Jeff turned his attention to the television, staring at the movie. He rocked back and forth in a trance, muttering and moaning beneath his breath. Tracy removed his shirt, and Jeff complimented him on his beauty, placing his head against the bare chest.

Dahmer eventually made his way to the kitchen to grab a beer. It was then Tracy shoved the knife underneath the bed, hiding it from view. Then Tracy walked out of the bedroom and told Jeff to trust him. He'd do whatever as long as the handcuffs were off. That was what Jeff wanted to hear: compliance. He went to the bedroom to get the handcuff key; that was when Tracy made his escape, rushing out of the apartment after punching Jeff. He chased after Edwards, grabbing his arm and begging him to come back. But Tracy threw him off and fled.

He had survived five hours with Jeffrey Dahmer.

Police Officers Rolf Mueller and Robert Rauth were patrolling through the streets nearby. A man waved them down. A handcuff hung off his left wrist, shaking as he moved his arm. They stopped the car and listened to him tell them about his encounter with some "freak." And all he wanted was to get the handcuffs off. The officers tried their keys first. It didn't unlock. Curious and wanting to help Edward, together they went to apartment 213.

Jeffrey heard the knocking and got up, answering the door. There were two officers and Tracy Edwards standing behind them. They asked about the key, which Jeffrey said must be in the bedroom. At first, he invited the officer to go in and look at himself but then suddenly, as if remembering what laid in wait, stopped him.

"Back off!" Officer Rauth said.

Inside the small bedroom, Mueller noticed the large knife beneath the bed, but even more horrifying was located in the dresser's top drawer. There, in plain sight, was Jeffrey's collection of polaroids, showing images of dismembered heads and body parts.Mueller scooped them up, examining the stills of gored torsos, heads sitting in sinks, and organs littered about. All the shots were clearly taken within the very walls of the apartment. He returned to the living room and showed them to Rauth.

"These are real pictures," he said.

A switch turned on within Dahmer as the scene played out, and he realized what was suddenly happening. Afraid and agitated, Jeff resisted when Rauth began to restrain him. He fought back in a wave of panic, and a second squad car was called to the scene.

It was 11:50 pm when Jeffrey was handcuffed, laying on the floor, defeated. Edwards told the police about the fridge, how he remembered seeing something when Dahmer had gone to fetch a beer earlier.

Mueller opened the door to find a cardboard box. Inside, Bradehoft's head stared back. Quickly, the refrigerator door was slammed shut, and the Criminal Investigation Bureau was called in.

Shortly after midnight, Jeffrey was hauled away in the back of the cop car, and his small museum of death and horror was crammed full of police and investigators who were left with the task of putting together the remains of a nightmare.

Confession

Lionel answered the phone while at home to find his mother concerned. Jeffrey hadn't shown up after he promised to stop by for a visit on July 22. He never called her.

The next day, Lionel phoned his son's apartment. The other line rang several times, then was answered by a stranger. He asked to speak with Jeff but was told he wasn't there at the moment.

"Where is he?" Lionel asked.

"Someone will call you, Mr. Dahmer."

"Call me?! About what?"

"A detective will call you."

It was then he learned that the detectives were investigating a homicide. Immediately, Lionel feared something had happened to Jeff. But the officer assured him that Jeff was indeed alive and well.

The night he was arrested was a hot, sweltering July night in the city. Within the first hour, police swarmed the apartment, and Jeffrey was taken away by Detective Kennedy to be questioned.

The inside of apartment 213 was sorted and sifted. Neighbors were awake and gathered in crowds to witness the scene. News reporters and media stood outside trying to be the first to break the story. And while the hours passed, the body count began to rise as police worked to put together the pieces. Seven skulls and four heads were counted. The first total came to eleven murdered individuals.

The fridge shelves had a head beside an opened box of baking soda, a poor attempt to stop the smell. Human meat had been frozen in the fridge as well. Beside it, in the freezer his father had asked about, three more heads were stored neatly in tied plastic bags. Two skulls were removed from a box that once contained a laptop, along with an album full of polaroids. Three skulls and with human bones were pulled out of the filing cabinet. The bedroom closet stored two human skulls, hands, and a penis. The blue drum was hauled out by men in yellow hazmat suits, its contents to be inspected.

At the station, Jeffrey was directed to a chair and told to sit down.

"You're not going to let them hit me anymore, are you?" he asked Detective Kennedy. The smell of alcohol and beer lingered on his breath and his speech was slightly slurred. Jeff was assured he wouldn't be hurt anymore, and right now, the detectives only wanted to talk. He was given a cup of coffee and a cigarette.

The interview began at 1:30 in the morning.

"What can you tell me about the guy in the refrigerator," Detective Kennedy asked. For the next six hours, Jeffrey confessed to killing seventeen men to Detective Kennedy and Murphy. He began when he was a child, slowly opening up about his crimes and dark desires. The two men could only sit and listen, stunned, and wonder how one man could commit so much evil.

Out of his seventeen victims, fourteen of them had been men of color; eleven were Blackmen. He stated these were not hate crimes; his only goal was "was to find the best looking guy that I could." But Jeff also understood black, gay men reported missing was not a priority of the Milwaukee police, and he knew his word would be trusted over his victims' if they were not white.

On July 25, 1991, Jeffrey Dahmer was charged with four counts of first-degree intentional homicide. Unshaven and defeated, he arrived in court with heavy bags beneath his eyes. His bail was set to one million dollars.

After the court hearing, Dahmer met with the detectives. They produced photos of those who'd been reported missing along with Dahmer's polaroids, desperate to identify his victims. They listened to him reveal more strange bits of his stories and the depth of his dark soul. All the while, Jeffrey smoked cigarette after cigarette, speaking of murder and rape with a cold, blank tone.

During the investigation, it became painstakingly clear that Jeffrey Dahmer was a complete loner. As the media storm spread throughout the country and world, people called in to tell stories about Jeff, but a pattern unfolded that, though they had stories, none were close to Jeff. No one had any insight into his life or his crimes. His sole goal was one dedicated to fleeting hedonistic desire, an empty and isolating pursuit. And it was fueled by alcohol. While locked away, Jeff occasionally grew shaky, but smoking and coffee helped him through the withdrawal.

When the victims were identified and his story recorded, it was left to his lawyer to build Jeff's defense before trial. Jeff waived the rights to the first trial to determine whether or not he was guilty and had no desire to contest anything. His attorney, Gerald Boyle, wanted to put Jeff inside a psychiatric hospital, where he'd receive better treatment for his mental health, instead of a prison. But nothing about Jeff's crimes proved insanity. He didn't hear voices or suffer from hallucinations; at a passing glance, he was a normal man. Detective Patrick Kennedy described, "You think of the crimes that he committed, they're so horrific you kinda think only a madman or somebody totally evil–evil incarnate would do this, but when you talked with Jeff Dahmer you did not get this idea. He could be engaging, he could be bright, witty, he could make jokes. He was able to fool a lot of people." He came off as far too normal for his murders to be chalked up to madness. Still, Boyle focused on building a case that centered around Jeff's murders and sexuality to paint a portrait of a man criminally insane. But the last thing Jeff wanted was to stand trial and have his mental state tested, even if it was his right to challenge his sanity in court.

"I see no hope. It's just completely hopeless from my standpoint. I'm not going to sit up in front of all those people and try to answer questions," Jeffrey said.

After identifying his victims and being told he could not write to his grandmother, there was little Jeffrey cared about. He thought death would be better than what he had to face now. Between the inability to drown himself in alcohol and the hours spent in jail, he was given time to reflect upon himself and his actions. He was guarded twenty-four hours in case he attempted suicide; the light of his cell was left on while he slept, and the bedbugs squirmed in the cot beneath him. Hours passed with nothing but perpetual boredom, but he had found relief in the confession and while speaking with psychiatrists and the police. The burden and secrets were removed; all that was left was the isolation and suffocating depression.

Jeffrey's family faced the onslaught of the media. Joyce attempted to go into hiding while Lionel and Shari faced the brunt of the attention. "I did not realize just how sick he was. I realize now that he is mentally ill, but I did not know the extent. And I will, as I always have, stand by him in my thoughts and prayers," Lionel stated in a brief television interview. And though Lionel stood fast by his son and offered support, Jeff's actions submerged him and Shari in their own nightmare that they desperately wanted to disassociate from.

Unfortunately, the massive publicity of the trial would forbid the Dahmers from having a normal life.

January 27, 1991, marked Dahmer's first day of his trial. The press and those gathered to witness all turned to watch Jeffrey Dahmer walk into the courtroom. He sat down silently, wearing a brown jacket and button-up. His signature aviator glasses had been left off on purpose. That way, he didn't have to see what was happening around him or who looked at him. He wanted nothing to do with his own trial, but endured it because he had no choice.

"This is a sad commentary. I take no delight in telling you this. I grieve for the family. I tell you these things because I must because you have to know," Gerald Boyle said, as he weaved together a narrative for the jury, attempting to persuade them that Jeffrey was very mentally ill. "This was not an evil man, this was a sick man."

Edward Michael McMann opened then in juxtaposition, painting a portrait of a man with uncontrolled sexual urges. He believed Jeffrey wasn't insane, quite the opposite. He was cunning and manipulative, using deceit when he needed it.

As the courtroom listened to the proposed sides, fighting to portray Dahmer in two different views, the defendant sat silently, occasionally rocking back and forth in his chair, showing little emotion. Witnesses were called to stand. The first was Detective Kennedy, who heard the confession. Tracy Edwards was soon to follow after Detective Murphy, who went through the evidence and photographs of the victims. Doctors and psychologists testified and were cross-examined.

It was the last witness, Dr. Park Dietz, who made one of the greatest impacts on understanding Jeffrey Dahmer. On February 12, he arrived at the courtroom. "Dahmer went to great lengths to be alone with his victim," he began, "and to have no witnesses." At first, it appeared an obvious statement, but Dietz went on listing out Jeffrey's routine of waiting until the weekends, obtaining sleeping pills, and preparing a cash offer. These were the signs of a man who planned and calculated his attacks, not signs of an insane person. There was also the fact that he needed alcohol to commit the murder. "If he had a compulsion to kill, he would not have had to drink alcohol. He had to drink alcohol to overcome his inhibition, to do the crime which he would rather not do." Dietz went through each murder in detail, going through whether Jeff had the ability to recognize right from wrong. It wasn't a disease or mental compulsion; it was a willing choice propelled by alcohol. And when he was finished, Gerald Boyle rose and asked Deitz if Jeffrey had stopped drinking, would the murder have stopped as well.

Everyone in the courtroom knew Jeff would have continued to murder if he had not been arrested that July, but what they didn't know was if it wasn't mental disease propelling him forward, what was?

During his closing statement, the silver-haired Gerald Boyle attempted one last time to humanize Jeff: "You know what happened. He threw in the towel. He just became helpless in his own mind. And I submit to you that at some juncture along this killing spree one would have to be blinded not to accept the fact that he was so out of control that he couldn't conform his conduct anymore. No human being on the face of the earth could do anything worse than what he did. Nobody could be more reprehensible than this man if he's sane. Nobody. The devil would be in a tie. But if he's sick—but if he's sick—then he isn't the devil."

McMann rose then to follow with him a stack of photos, each one a portrait of Dahmer's victims shown to the jury. "Don't forget Ernest Miller, who was stabbed to death by the defendant because he was becoming conscious . . . don't forget Curtis Straughter, strangled to death by the defendant . . . don't forget Jeremiah Weinberger, who struggled for life for a day and a half before he died at the hands of the defendant."

On Saturday, February 15, the court was gathered after the jury had reached a decision. The air was tense with anticipation. Judge Gram quickly scanned the document before him, then in a strong commanding voice read aloud what ten of the twelve jurors voted: "Sane on all counts."

Jeffrey sat, transfixed in silence.

"Jeffrey Dahmer, I hate you, you motherfucker. This is how you react when you're out of control!" Errol Lindsey's sister shouted as she lunged forward. "Satan, I hate you, Satan!" she continued as four deputies jumped to stop her and take her back to her seat.

Other family members stepped forward on Monday during the sentencing. Curtis Straughter's grandmother looked at Dahmer and told him, "You almost destroyed me. But I refuse to let you. I will carry on. " When the last of the family members spoke, Boyle stepped forward announcing Jeffrey himself wanted to speak.

The courtroom listened in silence to each of Jeff's words. He expressed his guilt and shame he brought upon his family, owning the blame for his crimes. He thanked his lawyer then read, "In closing, I just want to say that I hope God has forgiven me. I know society will never be able to forgive me. I know the families of the victims will never be able to forgive me. I promise I will pray each day to ask their forgiveness when the hurt goes away, if ever. I have seen their tears, and if I could give my life right now to bring their loved ones back, I would do it. I am so very sorry." He took his seat and received his sentence.

He was sentenced to life for each of his murders. In theory, Jeffrey Dahmer would serve over nine hundred years in prison.

He was taken away in a bright orange prison jumpsuit to spend the rest of his days at Columbia Correctional Institute in Portage, Wisconsin. Shari and Lionel hugged him farewell one last time. His new home was an isolated eight by ten-foot-long cell. At the beginning of his sentence, he was guarded and kept from the other prisoners for fear he might be killed. He spent much of his time reading books and magazines, keeping to himself. The first year in prison went without incident as he quickly conformed into a model inmate. He was allowed a few family visits, and finally, he was allowed monitored social interaction with the other prisoners.

He took opportunities to appear on television shows and be interviewed. While he was locked away, he'd become a legendary figure in America. Everyone knew about the cannibal killer, Jeffrey Dahmer. By the fall of 1993, restrictions lessened and Dahmer was eating in the communal setting with the other inmates. He was given work detail with two others, one of which was a black man named Christopher Scarver, who had schizophrenia and was serving life for murder.

November 28, 1993, at 7:50 am, Dahmer was escorted with Scarver and another inmate to the bathrooms. There they'd mop down the showers. As Dahmer started his daily task of cleaning, the guards left the dangerous men alone and unattended.

Twenty minutes passed.

The guards returned. Red blood ran over the tile floor, where Dahmer laid facedown in the pool of it. His head was crushed and he was unconscious. It appeared he'd had been slammed into the wall or floor multiple times. He was rushed to the emergency room along with another inmate who was also attacked by Scarver. Scarver revealed he had been disgusted with Jeffrey's crimes and kept a newspaper clipping detailing Dahmer's murders. "Some people who are in prison are repentant," Scarver said, "but he was not one of them."

At 9:11 am, Jeffrey Dahmer was pronounced dead.

References

Colin McMahon and Jerry Crimmins. Tribune reporters David Silverman. (2018, September 02). Victim left oak park to be with his fiance. Retrieved May 10, 2021, from https://www.chicagotribune.com/news/ct-xpm-1991-07-25-9103220686-story.html

Dahmer, L. (1994). *A father's story*. New York: W. Morrow &.

Davis, D. (1995). *The Jeffrey Dahmer story: An American nightmare*. New York: St. Martin's Paperbacks.

Kennedy, P., & Maharaj, R. (2016). *Dahmer detective: The interrogation and investigation that shocked the world*. Winnipeg: Poison Berry Press.

MASTERS, B. (2020). *SHRINE OF JEFFREY DAHMER*. HODDER PAPERBACK.

MPI Media Group. (2013). *The Jeffrey Dahmer files*. New York, NY: IFC Films.

Reports, T. (2019, May 23). Inmate goes public with why he KILLED serial murderer Jeffrey Dahmer. Retrieved May 10, 2021, from https://www.chicagotribune.com/news/breaking/ct-inmate-goes-public-with-why-he-killed-serial-murderer-jeffrey-dahmer-20150501-story.html

Rosewood, J. (2017). *Jeffrey Dahmer: A terrifying true story of rape, murder and cannibalism.* Lak publishing.

Schwartz, A. E. (2011). *The man who could not kill enough: The secret murders of Milwaukee's Jeffrey Dahmer.* Bloomington, IN: IUniverse.

Printed in Great Britain
by Amazon